You Must Revise Your Life

POETS ON POETRY

David Lehman, General Editor
Donald Hall, Founding Editor

William Stafford

You Must

Revise

Your Life

Ann Arbor
The University of Michigan Press

2009   2008   2007   2006   14   13   12   11

Library of Congress Cataloging-in-Publication Data

Stafford, William Edgar, 1914–
    You must revise your life.

    (Poets on poetry)
    1. Stafford, William Edgar, 1914–   —Interviews.
2. Poets, American—20th century—Interviews.
3. Poetry.   I. Title.   II. Series
PS3537.T143Z477   1986   821   86-16037
ISBN 0-472-09371-1 (alk. paper)
ISBN 0-472-06371-5 (pbk. : alk. paper)
ISBN 978-0-472-06371-0 (pbk. : alk. paper)

Acknowledgments

Grateful acknowledgment is made to the following individuals, organizations, journals, and publishers for permission to reprint previously published material.

ADE Bulletin, a publication of the Association of Departments of English, for "A Priest of the Imagination," originally published in *ADE Bulletin,* no. 76 (Winter 1983).

American Poetry Review for "Facing Up to the Job," which first appeared as "William Stafford: An Interview with Nancy Bunge" in *American Poetry Review* 10, no. 6 (November/December 1981).

Stephen Berg for "Breathing on a Poem," from *Singular Voices,* edited by Stephen Berg (New York: Avon Books, 1985).

Brockport Review for "Leaving a Writers' Conference," *Brockport Review,* no. 2 (1982).

Chicago Review for "Thinking about Being Called Simple by a Critic," *Chicago Review* 30, no. 3 (March 1979).

Christian Science Monitor for "When I Met My Muse," *Christian Science Monitor,* October 18, 1977; and for "Farewell at a Writers' Conference," *Christian Science Monitor,* May 5, 1982.

Suzanne Ferris for "Passwords," from *Passwords,* a packet of broadsides published February, 1980.

Field for "Burning a Book," *Field,* no. 31 (Fall 1984).

Gale Research Company for "William Stafford: 1914–" from *Contemporary Authors Autobiography Series,* vol. 3.

An Invitation to the Reader

Becoming a writer is just partly the learning of tricks and processes of language. Literature comes about by way of a behavior, a way of thinking, a tendency of mind and feeling.

We can all learn technique and then improvise pieces of writing again and again, but without a certain security of character we cannot sustain the vision, the trajectory of significant creation: we can learn and know and still not understand. Perceiving the need for that security of character is not enough—you have to possess it, and it is a gift, or something like a gift. You can't earn it, or calculate how to get it. But it may come, when you enter the life of writing with patience and trust. Dawn comes, and it comes for all, but not on demand.

What to do? In this book readers are invited to approach the composing of literature by several slanting ways, a number of them infrequently discussed—or infrequently discussed seriously and respectfully.

"Sources and Resources" is one of the slant ways, an account of one life in writing.

The way of writing in that life brought about some pieces that illuminate procedures; these pieces are in "Poems on Writing."

Where do poems come from?—a natural question, one often asked. Four pieces in this section address this topic.

Interviews often overlap and wander around, but sometimes they happen upon special insights. In "Glimpses of How It Is" three of those luckier interchanges spread out such topics as religion and writing, facing up to a complex of jobs, and the kind of living that makes a place your own and your writing a match for it.

The last section considers teaching and writing and performing—most writers get involved in this combination as teachers, as students, or at least as beneficiaries (or victims) of the results.

Contents

I

Sources and Resources

William Stafford: 1914–

My life in writing, or my life as a writer, comes to me as two parts, like two rivers that blend. One part is easy to tell: the times, the places, events, people. The other part is mysterious; it is my thoughts, the flow of my inner life, the reveries and impulses that never get known—perhaps even to me. This second part wanders along at its own pace, caught up in a story that touches the outward story but is not the same. Often this inner story hardly belongs to the place where I'm living. Whatever the calendar says, whatever outsiders demand, this other part of my life doubles back and becomes involved in its own chosen events.

My writings are current manifestations of that blending. My poems, especially, are not to my mind crafted objects but little discoveries in language that spring from the encounters between outer events and that unpredictable—and never sufficiently identified—mysterious river.

Start with the places. There was always an edge to town near our house, wherever it was, around Kansas in the twenties and thirties—Hutchinson, Wichita, Liberal, Garden City, El Dorado, Lawrence. Beyond that edge was adventure, fields forever, or rivers that wended off over the horizon forever. And in the center of town was a library, another kind of edge, out there forever, to explore.

Those Carnegie libraries packed with dynamite books, we raided them every week. My parents were not progressive—they did not try to encourage their kids (three of us, sister Peggy eighteen months younger than I, and brother Bob four years younger yet). No, my parents were jealous; they grabbed books first. My mother, when we were reading around through some anthology, passing it along, would insist on her favorite and resent my reading it before she had a chance. "Hats off! Along the street there comes a blare of bugles, a ruffle of drums!" How she hated it when I read that one ahead of her! And this despite her horror of militarism: she wouldn't let me join the Boy Scouts because of the uniform. Early I learned this disjunction between literature and life—my parents would luxuriate in stories they would be appalled to find linked to any of their own family. I remember my mother laughing till she cried when she read *Elmer Gantry,* though she was quite respectful of the clergy.

Another early favorite, and one among many that influenced me when World War II came, was about a "little boy named Gottlieb in a country far from our own." Germany came into my consciousness by way of such verses; I felt a pang of yearning and fellowship. One that my father read to us with great effect was "A Night with the Wolf"—"Little one, climb on my knee—hark how the rain is pouring over the roof in the pitchblack night and the wind in the chimney roaring!" How could we resist so exciting a story? I never got over it.

This territory of the book looms so much in our lives that it seems natural that we would write, engaging in the other half of the transaction. My father would try. He carried pieces around in his billfold, things he wrote, things I wrote. He was carrying "Annabel Lee" when he died. He was never a scholar, just addicted to reading—and to entering that realm from his side, too. When I was in third grade he brought home a set (was it four volumes?) of H. G. Wells's *The Outline of History*—he wanted to know all of it. Especially in looking at pictures of cave men and arrowheads, I raced through the set. I wanted our town to be wiped out, somehow, so that I could escape and survive in the woods alone. To be ready I buried a packet of fishhooks, string, and some matches down by the tracks—that one of us at least would have supplies for the long trek when disaster came.

At school during free time in the third grade I was writing

up a story of such an adventure, a journey into the North when winter was coming. Dillon Wallace, I think, was the writer influencing me at the time, maybe a story about "Ungava Bob," or "Tales of the Labrador." Once the teacher caught me at the writing and took my tablet. She read it over silently, then handed it back. No comment.

Besides the reading (and their talk—I always appreciated that), the first great aesthetic experience I remember with my parents was one weekend when my father brought home a shotgun. We would go duck hunting. The blue barrel, the shiny walnut stock: I stood admiring the gun where it stood in the corner. My father carefully handed it to me. He opened it and let me look out the long, deep, cool, mirrored barrel. He told me about walnut and how it was selected and made into gunstocks. My fingers roved along the grain. How smooth it was! Just as I thought of making a story when I read one, I thought of making a gunstock, selecting the tree, hacking out a form, polishing it. . . .

Before dawn we drove west to the Arkansas River—"The Big River," my father called it. Everything excited me, the dark, the cool air, the steady car. And the words that came: north of us was Great Bend, and around there Cheyenne Bottoms. On west was the salt marsh. Teal would be coming in, canvasbacks, buffleheads. In the early dark we crept through tall weeds, past mysterious trees. At first light long scarfs of ducks came in talking to each other as they dropped. The seething cattails and grasses whispered and gushed in the shadows. And the river was there, going on westward, past islands, along groves, into the wilderness, an endless world for exploring. I stop now and worship those times. The air was clear and sharp; no one was ahead of us; all was like in the first days of creation. We could wander all day, try to get lost, always able to take care of ourselves.

In later life other people, other writers, would talk to me about rebellion, about resentments against parents. My parents didn't fit the patterns I heard about. True, they had secrets, they established certain rules; but it all made sense. And they never pretended that I wouldn't have my own life, my own way of living. They stood to one side and watched. An example comes to me, from those very early times of hunting with my father.

We were out rambling the countryside, and we saw a hawk land in a cottonwood far across a field. When we got there we couldn't see it, and I stood waiting for my father to show me where it was. He said something that marked a phase of my life: "Bill, maybe your eyes are better than mine. Maybe you will be the one to see the hawk." This remark was not the only move he made of that kind, of course; but it sticks in my mind as an emblem. I was a partner; I verged on being grown-up. My father was contending, ready to win, ready to lose. And when my parents talked now, and understood each other about things beyond my understanding, maybe I could follow them. I listened, sometimes on the floorboards of an open car (we always seemed to be overloaded, grown-ups on seats, kids perched here and there). The big engine would rumble beside me, the snatches of talk and song come down where I was.

And song, yes. My parents and their friends sang in those days, things like "A Long, Long Trail Awinding," "Three O'clock in the Morning," "Swanee River." Everywhere our lives were surrounded by songs and stories and poems, and lyrical splurges of excited talk.

My mother loved gossip and spite. From her I learned the slant remark, the slight shift of expression that signaled a drop into several layers of speculation while someone pontificated. But she had the sentiment that fueled such readiness to read into talk and events. She loved old-time stories of the plains—Bess Streeter Aldrich was a favorite author, and Willa Cather. Fairy tales carried her away. She was lost for days in *Ben Hur,* and anything by Edna Ferber. My father read such things, fast. He wanted to understand. He explained the car, the wiring systems at home, new ideas like radio.

We all took up the annual anthologies of short stories and plays—this was in the thirties, the O. Henry Memorial Award pieces. We could recite from *Spoon River Anthology*—"Out of me unworthy and unknown," "We went to the dances at Chancellorsville," "Degenerate sons and daughters . . . it takes life to love life." We picked up anything at the library—the volumes I remember mostly had browned pages, scarred covers—Altsheler (Oh, Henry Ware, I wanted to follow you), Joseph C. Lincoln, Earnest Thompson Seton, and later Dickens, George Eliot (I never could turn against *Silas Marner* when high school teachers began to ridicule it), Kipling, Thornton Wilder, Robinson Jeffers. I think I began to know my way between English and American literature by the smell of the shelves—something about glue or paper, or maybe the musty holds of ships.

In the thirties our family along with all our neighbors coasted into the depression. There was a short time, as my father jumped from one short-term job to another, when our only cash was from my paper route. I remember cranking the old Plymouth and having the crank whip out of my hand and into the radiator, making a gash that water spouted from. It was a dismal moment—the starter already broken, no money to repair the car. During those times my mother was jealous of women with better clothes; and to her my sister—coming to bloom and able to attain some style even with the poorest materials—was a pride but also a rival.

Hopping for jobs for my father we moved from Hutchinson to Wichita, to Hutchinson, to Liberal, to Garden City, to El Dorado. Some stories of mine came out of those moves—"Answer Echoes," "The Osage Orange Tree" come to mind. And one experience too strange and fervent to become a story.

It was like an Indian vision-quest. I was in Liberal High School, and one autumn afternoon on a weekend I got on my bike with a camping pack (the sleeping bag was probably a blanket and safety pins) and rode ten or twelve miles to the Cimarron River northeast of town. I hid my bike and climbed into the breaks above the river. It is all open country, miles of red-brown brush and grass. A few cottonwoods and willows lined the river far down—maybe a mile—from me. On that still, serene day I stayed and watched. How slow and majestic the day was, and the sunset. No person anywhere, nothing, just space, the solid earth, gradually a star, the stars. Quail sounds, a coyote yapping.

In the middle of the night I woke and saw a long, lighted passenger train slowly pulling along across the far horizon. No sound. Steady stars. The morning was dim, sure, an imperceptible brightening of sky with yellow, gray, orange, and then the powerful sun. That encounter with the size and serenity of the earth and its neighbors in the sky has never left me. The earth was my home; I would never feel lost while it held me.

One job, the next spring, when I was in Garden City Junior College (my parents had moved there—it was part of my father's territory in his job with an oil company), I survived as my most extreme depression job. A classmate hired me to help in his truck garden. Neither of us could find another job; he would raise vegetables on a friend's acreage, and we would peddle them from door to door. He was hardworking and an enterpriser. My pay would be ten cents an hour—a dollar a day. Pretty good.

But the soil, out along a bench above the Arkansas River, was clay; the air was dry. We had a wheeled plow, but the dirt was too hard for one person to push. By rigging a harness, I was able to pull, and with Charlie pushing and me pulling we managed to break up that hardpan. By the end of a day of such work my legs would tremble uncontrollably—I have seen exhausted horses tremble like that. In the hot sun, straining for hours, we dragged along. Never did a drink of water taste so good.

We planted sweet potatoes, tomatoes, beans, but our crop was thin and of poor quality. Charlie never did come even on that job, and I did not get paid. My children have heard that story, about when Daddy was a mule.

In later years when applying for a job I usually left that one off my record, but I sometimes listed many others. One was working in the sugar beet fields. It was a stoop crop in those days; you used a hoe with a short handle for thinning, so as to be able to pluck out all but one plant at each location, about fourteen inches apart. Lunch hours were the best on that job: we could crawl under the Ford for shade and eat jelly sandwiches and gulp canteen water. The pay as I remember was five dollars an acre, and we did get paid—about five dollars a day. Wonderful!

One more job as a background for the writing—the oil refinery in El Dorado. After chopping weeds around the storage tanks, I graduated to electrician's helper. My boss was a kind, helpful man. But our job reinforced my sense of how the world was beginning to be among people (World War II was huffing in the wings). The air where we worked was so volatile that we knew any spark could risk an explosion. Our environment, like everyone's today, was risky. We had to take thought, even about familiar, routine moves: turning on a switch or swinging an iron hammer could be the last move. Later, when feelings were high even among friends, I felt like that during the war while I was a conscientious objector.

But first, and a big move toward becoming a writer, was a spell at college, the University of Kansas. With sixty dollars at the beginning of school I could make it through the year: a few dollars for fees, maybe ten for books, some for the beginning of rent. Then I worked for room and board, serving tables at a residence hall, making beds, roaming the registration lines for students to stay at my employer's place.

Several new experiences in my first move away from a hometown began to influence my writing. One was just the usual in college days—girls, social life. A teacher in phys. ed. taught dancing some evenings, and I learned enough to get along. The landlady's daughters, two jittery, generous good sports, would help me wash up the dishes in time for the weekly dances at the best places—Westminster Foundation, Wesley Club, anywhere. We were truly ecumenical. Oh, Georgia, Rachel, Agnes. . . . My fervency and understanding increased, I think, in my writings at that time.

And it is strange how experiences blend and enhance each other. Once in the evening in the library something happened that linked to my dream-vision night along the Cimarron, and again it was a combination of influences. It was winter; a strange, violet light was in the sky—a color typical of clear prairie evenings when the air is freezing. Something about the light, and the quiet library, and my being away from home—many influences at once—made me sit and dream in a special way. I began to write. What came to me was a poem, with phrases that caught the time, my feelings. I was as if in a shell that glowed. All the big, dim reading room became more itself and had more meaning because of what I was writing. The alcove at the east end where the literature-browsing books were (a favorite place of mine) was darker and more velvety. My steps, walking back to the boarding house to work, were ritual steps, feet placed carefully on the storybook world.

My writing picked up momentum in those years in Lawrence, the town where the University of Kansas is; my habit of daily writing began, and the other river, the second main strand of my writing, began to put a strain on the flow of events around me.

It was like this. Professor Margaret Lynn held a creative writing class at her home. She knew how to write; she had written books. She would read what I brought. And every week I had a day, just before her late-afternoon class, to write. My stories about Liberal and Garden City and El Dorado began to crystallize. For me, they glowed on the page.

But the stories and the poems no longer tracked along with the outer events that came from recollection: history was stalking us, and my role in the life around me took a twist that was to make a great difference. One part of the strain was the emerging certainty of World War II. Our professors predicted it in class after class, and one of them, John Ise, in economics, firmly warned us. Another part of the strain was a sense of wanting to protest on campus; there were customs that hurt. Some of us would go into the café at the Union and have a sit-in, to break down the policy against serving blacks—"Negroes," in those days. The Union policy was that segregation must be preserved. Any student could order, but whites and blacks could not sit together and be served. So we would sit apart, be served, then take our food and sit down together. I didn't have to be black to be bitter about it.

My part in this kind of social action was a new feeling for me. I found myself most in sympathy with the program of the Fellowship of Reconciliation (other groups were taking part in such actions, but with different backgrounds and goals— the FOR was pacifist, and that fit my feelings). Various kinds of splinter groups began to be active: socialists, the Young Communist League, religious organizations with their own programs. One classmate went off to the war in Spain and was killed. It was a time of great excitement and turmoil, especially for someone like me from a background little prepared—except for reading—for the swirl of opinions and actions. That reading and the life of my parents combined to give me a certain angle of vision about it all: official acts like that of the student union in its segregation policy did not appeal; joining an assortment of elements in Spain didn't either. "A Night with the Wolf," the little boy named Gottlieb "in a country far from our own" came back to me, and my mother's feelings about the uniforms of the Boy Scouts, and my night on the Cimarron envisioning the whole round earth.

Then I stood in the Union on the floor above the segregated café and heard President Roosevelt speak about "the day of infamy." We students looked at each other. It had come. And within two weeks, carrying a copy of *The Journal of John Woolman* given me by my landlady, I was on my way to a camp for conscientious objectors in Arkansas.

My four years of "alternative service under civilian direction" turned my life sharply into that independent channel of the second river—a course hereafter distinguished from any unexamined life, from the way it might have been in any of my hometowns. When I was released in 1946, a fictionalized but true-in-spirit account of that four years, called *Down in My Heart*, became my master's "creative thesis" at the University of Kansas and was published, my first book. In it are scenes that give the flavor and drama of those times for COs. The special influence of that four years on my writing deserves a glance here.

Because we had to work hard in the camps where I was—in Arkansas and around in California—we would be too tired for reading, writing, and study late in the evening. So some of us formed a group to use the "library" (a barracks where we put our books together), for early morning literary activity. We would quietly get up at four A.M. or so and make our way to the gathering place, where we could read and write till breakfast call. Then we would work all day outside—U.S. Forest Service work or soil conservation—and drag back to camp and into bed. We gained alert hours for mental work and the rest of the day for work required of us. Since those days, I have had the habit of writing in the early morning. That dawn time is precious: the world is quiet; no one will interrupt; you are rested and ready.

Even later when our four children were young, I found that time available. When one would waken hungry at four, I could get up at three. When they got old enough to be lazy again, I could drop back to a later hour, like four. Once our youngest found that Daddy was getting up early; lest he be lonely, she got up early to keep him company. She soon got over that.

And life as a conscientious objector in a popular war was an intensive lesson in certain ways to live. We were schooled early and often in the reasons and arguments for social action, or inaction: we found ourselves postgraduates in issues that most people considered only on occasion and amid like-minded people. We were surrounded by challenges that had to do with that tension between open, ordinary daily life and the interior life that distinguishes individuals from each other. The two parts of my life that blended or clashed in making my writing were in constant alertness. I felt my mornings as maintenance work or repair work on my integrity.

Hardly any statement or question looked cut-and-dried to me anymore. Even two plus two equals four took on a shimmer—isn't that a kind of Republican statement?

After the war, after the partners in Europe had jostled for their lines of settlement, after the atom bomb, COs were released at about the same rate as those in the armed services; and my wife and I found ourselves free to go where we wanted, to find jobs. (My pay during the four years was $2.50 a month, for stamps, soap, and such.)

My wife, yes—the daughter of a minister for the Church of the Brethren—and I met in 1943 at a CO camp outside of Santa Barbara. Within the year we were married. It was possible for her to live near, teaching in public schools; and we could have weekends and occasional leaves together. With my release we could establish a home.

My habit of early morning writing stayed and became confirmed through many moves and jobs in the next few years—southern California where the two of us taught in public schools, the San Francisco area (high school teaching had been hard) where I worked for Church World Service, a relief agency (staffed generously at that time by released COs). I remember one of my first checks for a poem during those years, from *Poetry* for something about a supermarket.

A big break came then, a teaching job at Lewis and Clark College in Portland, Oregon. The president of the school came through California for recruits and hired a CO and a Japanese, two types still in need in those days—1948—of a little shelter. My wife Dorothy and I were elated; we moved north and stayed—with brief excursions to teach (both of us) elsewhere—for thirty years or so.

One excursion made a big difference: we went to Iowa City for two years to get me a writing degree. Those years (1950–52) marked my first sustained relation to other writers. I was thirty-six and had written many poems and stories.

Paul Engle was head of the program at the University of Iowa. Verlin Cassell was teaching there, and Walter Clark, and a succession of others, some for visits, some for extended stays: Robert Penn Warren, Randall Jarrell, Reed Whittemore, Karl Shapiro. Those two years remain the principal reference point I have for the literary life as lived by others, though I have taught at writers' conferences for years and thus have had passing contacts. But at Iowa it was daily, intense, enlightening. I enjoyed Engle's free and easy manner, coming in with an armload of manuscripts and quipping as he came. I followed Clark around to listen to his sociability and his stories.

My background, that other river of my life, put me in a different situation from that of most others. I was older, and a CO, and married, with children (two by then). And the analytical habits of four years in camp persisted. There was a party; it was joyous; everyone talked and laughed a lot. My reaction was a poem submitted to the workshop.

At the Chairman's Housewarming

Talk like a jellyfish can ruin a party.
It did: I smiled whatever they said,
all the time wanting to assert myself
by announcing to all, "I eat whole wheat bread."

The jelly talk stole out on the cloth
and coated the silver tine by tine,
folding meek spoons and the true knifeblades
and tolling a tentacle into the wine.

And my talk too—it poured on the table
and coiled and died in the sugar bowl,
twitching a last thin participle
to flutter the candle over its soul.

Nothing escaped the jellyfish,
that terror from seas where whales can't live
(he could kill sharks by grabbing their tails
and neither refusing nor consenting to give).

Oh go home, you terrible fish;
let sea be sea and rock be rock.
Go back wishy-washy to your sheltered bay,
but let me live definite, shock by shock.

Paul Engle called me in after class: "I'm not like that!" "I know," I responded, "and I'm not either. It's just a poem, just a reaction." We talked it over, and he had ideas about revisions.

It was only after some years, after I tried to teach creative writing myself, that I began to formulate my distinctions about the process of writing. Those ideas became my second prose book, *Writing the Australian Crawl*. My disquiets—my pacifist disquiets I guess—about teaching and writing by competitive methods are scattered around in that book. For me, a crucial sentence there is this: "A writer is not so much someone who has something to say as he is someone who has found a process that will bring about new things he would not have thought of if he had not started to say them."

Part of my disquiet was that people were trying to write good poems and stories; that is, they were learning from each other about techniques. They were even reading in order to find out how to do it. Sacrilege! A novel read for a lesson is not a novel. I was still caught up in the dizziness, the enthusiasm of reading, the way we were at home, when we wanted to be taken out of ourselves. And in my own writing I was still just allowing the collisions of life to stir me into that delicious enjoyment of the other self as it encountered the products of time. Students who competed were not allowing themselves to write their way and explore that area of creative tension where the actual material of art guides the active artist.

Sometimes that exploration harmonized with someone else's needs or appetites. Sometimes not. But I wanted never to adjust my explorations to the anticipated expectations of others. Writing was enjoyable for the reverberation I got out of it, and the reverberation had to be discovered, not planned.

The pace of my daily writing and my devotion to whim brought many various poems through the fifties. Most of those poems never met anyone else's eyes, but an average of fifty were in the mail to editors all through the fifties, sixties, and seventies. Because my writing was an ongoing linking of the inner river of my life to the emergent realizations that daily experience brought, I was never without material. It seemed that even if I wrote as fast as I could I would never catch up with my life.

Mixed among my many rejections and a few acceptances (all through my life rejections have been at least four-fifths ahead of acceptances) were some experiences that had lasting effects. One was an especially coercive acceptance. A man named Richard Ashman, a doctor, started the *New Orleans Poetry Journal*. He published such little-known (at least to me) poets as Donald Hall and Galway Kinnell. He was a generous man; I remember that if he accepted something he would be so eager for me to get the check—small, but significant—that he would put an extra stamp on the return envelope (airmail took extra postage in those days). And for one of my poems he wrote a second, a most reassuring, acceptance afterward: "I looked at the current issue and just wanted to say how glad I am to have published your 'Thinking for Berky.'"

Encounters with editors like this one began to hearten me, and to establish an attitude that became important. For me, editors were friends who helped keep you from publishing what you shouldn't publish. They were not fierce guards set up to prevent recognition for new writers. So I wrote recklessly and left decisions about publishing to others. And even this early, and still sometimes in need of guidance, I fell into the habit of not showing my writings to anyone but editors. My wife and children knew that I was out in the garage-study typing away, but they didn't see the product, unless by chance, later, if it got published and happened to fall into their reading. It was never my practice to try out a piece of writing on anyone. The poems got changed or revised—if they did get changed, as a result of my continued interest— only by my own re-visioning of them.

How do these stray poems get into a book? As more and more accumulated in my file, after magazine publication, I began to think about that. In the late fifties, as I recall, I began to send a collection loosely approximate to what I had submitted at the Iowa Workshop for my degree. That bundle went to the University of Montana Press, to the University of Indiana Press, and I believe to other places. Editors were kind but not ready. Then during a year when I taught at San Jose State a librarian there named Robert Greenwood told me he was starting the Talisman Press and would like to look at my work. I hesitated, for I was thinking by then of big publishers, but maybe I would be in limbo about these poems if I didn't get rid of them. Greenwood and his partner Newton Baird published my first collection, *West of Your City*, in a beautiful edition of a few hundred. This was in 1960, and I was forty-six years old.

Since that time, a new book has naturally come ripe for me. I say "naturally" because for me a book has always been something that grew and declared itself. I sometimes take a spread of a hundred or so poems that have been in magazines and put them in groups around on the living room rug, so that I can begin to understand any relations they may have. Maybe some could be beginning poems; I let them get together. Some might be later; they go over there. A few begin to seem like stunts of some kind. This stack usually gets higher and higher. Some may be sad, some happy. I try to keep them from being unhelpful to each other, and usually they get into sections so as to make it easy to think about sequences. Finally there is an order, and a publisher gets a manuscript with a tentative table of contents plus some extra poems, and my word that I am ready to add, delete, or whatever. Almost always a publisher has a few ideas, and I have always acceded; for once a reader has a preference I find myself understanding that preference. And after all, I have plenty of poems.

People have told me that my way is spineless and slovenly. And I understand that point of view, but there are considerations deriving from my way of writing. Each piece comes to me as a crystallization of its own, and preferably without my thinking of its effect on others. It is true, though, that once a piece is done I have ideas about whether it might get a friendly reception from an editor or reader—from someone not entering it as I do, from the inside, from its relation to my continuing track through the maze of adjusting parts of my life. And for a poem the signs of its being negotiable in the market are fairly neat and clear. For instance, readers do not like to extend credit to poets: a poem must have early rewards. It must be eventful in language; there must be early and frequent verbal events. Content, or topic, is not nearly enough, of course. A poem is an experience in the reading or hearing; the eventfulness of a poem comes in the experience of the reader. And in those events for the reader there must be coherence; one experience must relate to and enhance the next, and so on. Readers should not be loaded with more information and guidance than a lively mind needs—puzzlement can be accepted, but insulting clarity is fatal to a poem.

These opinions about writing spilled over into my teaching. At first I taught as those around me did—correcting papers, pushing students to "succeed." But gradually my ways changed. A teacher just retiring at San Jose State had told me that teaching composition got harder and harder. She was writing more on a student's paper than the student had written. She was heroic. But I thought mistakenly so.

My classes became more like ballet than like workshops. What did a piece of writing mean?—not what did it say, but what did it portend, or hint, or reveal, about that surely valid human impulse that brought it about? My job was not to correct but to understand and participate. A student's paper was a test for me, and I began not to put any evaluation remarks at all on a paper. My remarks were meant to show my accompaniment, sometimes my readiness to learn more.

And finally I began to realize that I was just getting around to treating other people's writings the way I had always treated my own—as exercises and revelations about the convergence of the two rivers in anyone's life.

In the late fifties and henceforward for two decades, events in the world made a turn that brought my CO experience into play again: the Vietnam War carried poets right into the action on campuses where agitating was news. Readings had already begun to be popular as poetry began to prove available for bringing audiences together on issues the people felt to be important. And I took part—Kent State, Stanford, Berkeley, Madison, all over the country. I found myself zigzagging from Alaska to Florida to Hawaii to Maine to countries overseas. Everyone knows that those were strange times, but for me they were a special mixture. With my war surplus haversack over my shoulder, I was part of the student scene; but my coat and necktie linked me to faculty, to administration, even. And I felt loyalties both ways. I remember being welcomed at a protest rally on the Stanford campus some time in the late sixties. But I was disquieted when students raced across the campus (past laboratories where I could see science majors carefully measuring chemicals) into the president's office, throwing out chairs and cushions, and yelling insults at all administrators.

My grounds for being welcomed by students were odd,

too. World War II would have been supported by most of those around me; most activists were not pacifists but were political partisans, many of them ready for violence. That violence, it seemed to me, helped bring on the Nixon reaction. Both sides spread out leaving pacifists where they usually were, alone.

Another little quirk isolated me, a reluctance to put my writing to work for any cause. When leaders and prophets were poets who spoke to the condition of people, it was assumed that writers would engage with issues. And when preachers and philosophers sought for justice and compassion, it was assumed that language was for guidance, for heartening people. But in our time an artist could be carrying on something like an experiment, a free kind of juggling, and I liked that. In writing I felt free—no obligations.

When I looked at my writing, though, it proved to be full of issues, positions, and attempted wisdom. Poems were cautiously and indirectly, but definitely, advocacy writings, humanitarian statements often. Usually, when solicited for a poem that would help a cause, I found one. Peace poems, pity poems, allegiance poems—there they were. Setting off freely in my writing, I found myself again and again taking principled stands on religion, peace, sobriety, responsibility. How could I account for the wayward principles (or lack of being principled) and the dedicated product?

I speculate that when you relax, your real self, or the self you accept as yours, takes over; and for me that self had been so formed that my poems were respectful of religion, people, and ideas that were different. I felt like a wide-ranging scout, but I usually drifted into a certain kind of territory.

My reading reflected this, my customary reading, the kind I gravitated toward without regard to my career needs or the urgencies of advertising around me. Pascal was a favorite, and John Henry Newman. Several traveling circuits found me carrying Nietzsche paperbacks; he struck me as delightful, one of the funniest writers I could find. I remember once carrying *Zarathustra* up a mountain above Squaw Valley, on a sunny day when we had time off from the writers' conference there, and looking out between paragraphs to delight in just being in so spacious and varied a world, taking in the sun, the space, and the sense of wonderful leaps in the book in my hand.

These adventures are common I suppose, but they helped me perceive the greatness of literature, the widening of life possible for readers and writers. In school the spirit of our times and the prevalent biases of my teachers had channeled me, but the reaches of any library beckoned and teased my mind. It became suffocating to have only *For Whom the Bell Tolls* as a guide to the war in Spain (as it apparently was to many of my friends)—there must be thousands of adherents to views that I did not usually meet. Surely intelligent people who had outlandish views might be understood. I turned from historical positions offered me and tried alternatives—instead of Thomas Paine I read Edmund Burke, and loved it. I felt cheated by those who had decided for me that Paine had the truth.

However limited my expectations had been, or remained, and however pathetic these lunges of mine for perspectives, my searches in reading were part of my way of writing: my ambition was to explore in all directions, and in my own mind I was wildly experimental and irresponsible. If something occurred to me, I welcomed it. Wherever the muse looked, I jumped. I felt the tang of possibility; I even experimented with the wild bitter flavor of being a book burner. It seemed to me that living in a free country and not testing foregone conclusions would be a loss in anyone's life.

It was only far along in my teaching and writing—in the last ten years of my teaching, say, when I was deliberately withdrawing to half-time so as to save precious hours for writing—that I began to understand my way as simply incompatible with that of most others. It became apparent that many teachers, for instance, have forgotten how material begins to seek its own form, how a piece of wood, for instance, may like a certain curve when you are carving a gunstock like the one I admired in the corner of our living room, how a phrase when you speak it or write it begins to call up another phrase, or how a word suddenly finds another word that its syllables like to associate with.

For me an artist is someone who lets the material talk back. A relationship with the material is the distinction an artist has. And in my writing and teaching that "talking back" element became more and more important. I began to treat each encounter with a student as an occasion for learning as well as possible where the student was, how the material of the course was striking an individual. If I could find the periphery of a student's relation to a story, or how a phrase of my own had the impulse to join another phrase, I was ready for next steps. But this procedure required my listening in class or in conference, and my readiness to adjust my next move as a result of what I found out. And in writing, any snag in the language, even, became a signal for a move on my part. Writing was in its language aspect a series of moves like dancing. Imposing my will on language—or on a student, or on the citizens of a country—was not my style. I wanted to disappear as teacher, as writer, as citizen—be "the quiet of the land," as we used to designate ourselves in CO camps.

After I retired from teaching in 1978 I thought I would write more, but the poems have been happening along at about their usual pace. I get up early and have that precious time. Those quiet mornings bring the feeling that there is a tide, or what makes the tide, something you miss if people interrupt, or if there is noise where you live or in the kind of life you live. Even the kindest friend would jar that faint, delicious message you are receiving: something is offering you a guidance available only to those undistracted by anything else.

I can look back to that child read to by parents, led by the times and the developing self into intricate negotiations with language. I can cast back over this account of that child and have a great urge to revise, not the account (though I glimpse troubling implications there), but the life itself. Too late for that. As has happened all through my years, a poem brings alive my peculiar views and reticences—and maybe an experience that others can feel:

Ask Me

Some time when the river is ice ask me
mistakes I have made. Ask me whether
what I have done is my life. Others
have come in their slow way into
my thought, and some have tried to help
or to hurt: ask me what difference
their strongest love or hate has made.

I will listen to what you say.
You and I can turn and look
at the silent river and wait. We know
the current is there, hidden, and there
are comings and goings from miles away
that hold the stillness exactly before us.
What the river says, that is what I say.

II

Poems on Writing

Poems on Writing

Run Before Dawn

Most mornings I get away, slip out
the door before light, set forth on the dim, gray
road, letting my feet find a cadence
that softly carries me on. Nobody
is up—all alone my journey begins.

Some days, it's escape—the city is burning
behind me, cars have stalled in their tracks,
and everybody is fleeing like me but some other
    direction—
my stride is for life, a far place.

Other days, it is hunting—maybe some game will cross
my path and my stride will follow for hours, matching
all turns. My breathing has caught the right beat
for endurance; familiar trancelike scenes glide by.

And sometimes it's a dream of motion—streetlights
    coming near,
passing, shadows that lean before me, lengthened
then fading, and a sound from a tree—a soul, or an
    owl.

These journeys are quiet. They mark my days with
    adventure
too precious for anyone else to share, little gems
of darkness, the world going by, and my breath, and
    the road.

Near

Talking along in our not quite prose way
we all know it is not quite prose we speak,
and it is time to notice this intolerable snow
innumerably touching, before we sink.

It is time to notice, I say, the freezing snow
hesitating toward us from its gray heaven;
listen—it is falling not quite silently
and under it still you and I are walking.

Maybe there are trumpets in the houses we pass
and a redbird watching from an evergreen—
but nothing will happen until we pause
to flame what we know, before any signal's given.

You and Art

Your exact errors make a music
that nobody hears.
Your straying feet find the great dance,
walking alone.
And you live on a world where stumbling
always leads home.

Year after year fits over your face—
when there was youth, your talent
was youth;
later, you find your way by touch
where moss redeems the stone;

And you discover where music begins
before it makes any sound,
far in the mountains where canyons go
still as the always-falling, ever-new flakes of snow.

After Arguing against
the Contention That Art
Must Come from Discontent

Whispering to each handhold, "I'll be back,"
I go up the cliff in the dark. One place
I loosen a rock and listen a long time
till it hits, faint in the gulf, but the rush
of the torrent almost drowns it out, and the wind—
I almost forgot the wind: it tears at your side
or it waits and then buffets; you sag outward. . . .

I remember they said it would be hard. I scramble
by luck into a little pocket out of
the wind and begin to beat on the stones
with my scratched numb hands, rocking back and
      forth
in silent laughter there in the dark—
"Made it again!" Oh how I love this climb!
—the whispering to stones, the drag, the weight
as your muscles crack and ease on, working
right. They are back there, discontent,
waiting to be driven forth. I pound
on the earth, riding the earth past the stars:
"Made it again! Made it again!"

At This Point on the Page

Frightened at the slant of the writing, I looked up
at the student who shared it with me—
such pain was in the crossing of each *t,*
and a heart that skipped—lurched—in the loop of the *y.*
Sorrowing for the huddled lines my eyes had seen—
the terror of the *o*'s and *a*'s, and those draggled *g*'s,
I looked up at her face,
not wanting to read farther, at least by prose:
the hand shook that wrote that far on the page,
and what weight formed each word, God knows.

When I Met My Muse

I glanced at her and took my glasses
off—they were still singing. They buzzed
like a locust on the coffee table and then
ceased. Her voice belled forth, and the
sunlight bent. I felt the ceiling arch, and
knew that nails up there took a new grip
on whatever they touched. "I am your own
way of looking at things," she said. "When
you allow me to live with you, every
glance at the world around you will be
a sort of salvation." And I took her hand.

A Writer's Fountain Pen Talking

I gave out one day and left a woman
tied to a railroad track.

And what happened next?

The train couldn't go on; it stopped with a
foot in the air, like Napoleon's horse on the bridge
when it knew the plank was gone.

What ever happened?

When they filled the pen again—this was years later—
the train backed up, and an old woman
climbed on: she had waited all that time
to be rescued, or killed. She felt cheated,
for that strange diversion.

Where is she now?

Right here on this page, hiding in the ink you see.

Farewell at a Writers' Conference

As you go out, notice the barrel by the door.
It is for whatever you'd like to discard—those claims
you accepted for a while from someone forceful or
    loud
but not really your cup of tea, those heavy opinions
balanced on fragile foundations in arguments.

We invite you to retain your tickets for noticing
    things—
how sunlight is wide and democratic, how the rain
doesn't care who you are, how sounds will follow you
    home
and become songs that play back whenever you want
    them to.
A crow, a gull, a foghorn—keep these for your
    dreams.

Passwords

Might people stumble and wander
for not knowing the right words,
and get lost in their wandering?

Should you stand in the street
answering all passwords
day and night for any stranger?

You couldn't do that.
But sometimes your words
might link especially to some other person. . . .

Here is a package,
a program of passwords.
It is to bring strangers together.

Practice

When you stop off at rehearsal you can stumble
and still be forgiven. Your shadow practices. A light
says, "Good, good," where the piano meditates
with its wide grin, maintaining order as usual
but already trembling for time to go again.

Outside the hall a monstrous Oregon night
moans with its river of wind. It stumbles. Lights
flicker, and your shadow joins everything that ever
failed in the world, or triumphed unknown, alone,
wrapped in that secret mansion where genius lives.

Maybe it is all rehearsal, even when practice
ends and performance pretends to happen in the light
that remembers more than it touches, back through all
the rows and balcony tiers. Maybe your stumbling
saves you, and that sound in the night is more than
    the wind.

Thinking about Being
Called Simple by a Critic

I wanted the plums, but I waited.
The sun went down. The fire
went out. With no lights on
I waited. From the night again—
those words: how stupid I was.
And I closed my eyes to listen.
The words all sank down, deep
and rich. I felt their truth
and began to live them. They were mine
to enjoy. Who but a friend
could give so sternly what the sky
feels for everyone but few learn to
cherish? In the dark with the truth
I began the sentence of my life
and found it so simple there was no way
back into qualifying my thoughts
with irony or anything like that.
I went to the fridge and opened it—
sure enough the light was on.
I reached in and got the plums.

Burning a Book

Protecting each other, right in the center
a few pages glow a long time.
The cover goes first, then outer leaves
curling away, then spine and a scattering.
Truth, brittle and faint, burns easily,
its fire as hot as the fire lies make—
flame doesn't care. You can usually find
a few charred words in the ashes.

And some books ought to burn, trying for character
but just faking it. More disturbing
than book ashes are whole libraries that no one
got around to writing—desolate
towns, miles of unthought in cities,
and the terrorized countryside where wild dogs
own anything that moves. If a book
isn't written, no one needs to burn it—
ignorance can dance in the absence of fire.

So I've burned books. And there are many
I haven't ever written, and nobody has.

R_X Creative Writing: Identity

You take this pill, a new world
springs out of whatever sea
most drowned the old one,
arrives like light.

Then that bone light belongs
inside of things. You touch
or hear so much *yourself*
there is no dark.

Nothing left but what Aquinas
counted: he—touched, luminous—
bowed over sacred worlds, each one
conceived, then really there—

Not just hard things: down on
a duck as real as steel.
You know so sure there burns
a central vividness.

It tells you;
all you do is tell about it.

Every Morning All Over Again

Only the world guides me.
Weather pushes, or when it entices
I follow. Some kind of magnetism
turns me when I am walking
in the woods with no intentions.

There are leadings without any
reason, but they attract;
if I find there is nothing to gain
from them, I still follow—their power
is the power of the surrounding world.

But things that promise, or those
that will serve my purposes—they
interfere with the pure wind
from nowhere that sustains a kite,
or a gull, or a free spirit.

So, afloat again every morning,
I find the current: all the best
rivers have secret channels that
you have to find by whispering
like this, and then hear them and follow.

III

Where Do Poems
Come From?

Where "Yellow Cars" Comes From

Yellow Cars

Some of the cars are yellow, that go
by. Those you look at, so glimmering
when light glances at their passing. Think
of that hope: "Someone will
like me, maybe." The tan ones
don't care, the blue have made
a mistake, the white haven't tried.
But the yellow—you turn your head:
hope lasts a long time if you're happy.

Writing a poem is easy, like swimming into a fish trap. Analyzing a poem is hard, like swimming out of a fish trap. In casting back through the experience of having "Yellow Cars," I would like to find my way into what happened along in the writing, the easy part, the process that finds its way by accommodating to emerging experiences. And then I'd like to try to account for the fish trap pattern that one can reconstruct, rationally, the hard way, swimming out.

In early April of 1980 I was on a reading circuit, and of course kept on writing a little each day. The pages from that time give me little hints of a current that turned out to be on the way to this poem. On April 4 I find two stray jottings:

My room has light, and I
    am for the light, but when
that light goes wandering, my
    thought makes another room
where light can lead me home.

> My vial of anti-light pours a path
> for my shadow.

On April 8, among many jottings, I find this:

> Some time you look from your window
> into storm, cold, dark. It is warm
> where you are. Some day it will be home out there.

On April 10, strangely positioned amid another kind of sequence, is this:

> Mostly it is right, when a word goes by,
> to turn my head and watch it go into
> someone else's ear and let them answer.

Then, on April 12, I find, sprung amid other jottings, an essentially complete passage that became "Yellow Cars," with spooks of phrases from earlier passages in April:

> Some of the cars are yellow, that go
> by. Those I follow, so hurried are they
> when light allows their passing. Think
> of that optimism: "Someone will
> like me, maybe." The black ones
> don't care, the blue have made
> a mistake, the white haven't entered.
> But the yellow—I turn my head:
> hope lasts a long time, if you're happy.

Now, was this poem written in a few minutes—the version above—on April 12? Or was it written, jerkily, blunderingly, but with never-faltering direction, by means of writing experiences (and other experiences) that were happening along to me all during several weeks of April 1980? Either way, I could live with the choice, but the second way is the one that seems to me more helpful in considering how a piece of art *arrives*.

It would be endless to prowl through the influences and the characteristic turns I feel in this poem; but staying a long way short of that kind of excursion I want to consider certain perceptible trends as the poem unfolded. And then will come my turn toward considering the poem as a set of strategies.

About this poem, from the insi
and quiet as it is—it reverberates
most strongly held life commitment.
ridiculously quiet and insultingly clea
relevance. It offers readers or hearers
tossed aside, if they are dumb enough
deserve, and there is a mean part of me ι
have what they impetuously claim for the
continues to assert undeniable, but perha
tions—but perhaps not trivial. And the expe   ¸eading
the poem is itself not an experience of attain ¸or not attain-
ing worthy statements, but an experience of taking a roller
coaster of offerings, withholdings, little giddy turns, and then
a closure that suddenly welds together what the whole poem
has been tending toward.

Or so I see it. Small as it is, quiet as it is, I'll take my stand
with the sound it makes when struck to test its completeness
and tone after it is finished.

Now, to swim out of the fish trap—to seek patterns or tactics
that seem to carry this little package out of ordinary *message*
and into poetry—I stare at the finished poem. It doesn't spin
its wheels, make claims for itself, overrun its demonstrations;
that is, it eases the reader into an experience that does not
require giving credit to the writer or bracing oneself to ad-
mire. But it does begin at once to have various little bonuses
in the telling.

It spills along, line by line, roving downward, till it gets to
the last three end-stopped lines, where conclusions begin to
happen. The trajectory of the poem is smooth-onward, then
staccato as it drives home. I believe I was led to this pattern
from just following opportunities that came to me; but once
the opportunities come along, they are embraced. The "revi-
sion" process is largely a process of accepting what one can
from the given, and then of politely declining and selecting
among alternatives when it feels right to do so.

The persona in this poem, it seems to me, begins to be easy
and a little deprecatory—and then stays that way. There is
sympathy for our humanness, a general participation feeling;

...at inheres in being a participant in human-
...ed by the speaker. By the end of the poem what is
... is not much, but it is undeniable; and something as
...ural as choosing a color one likes becomes like a banner
for the life force.

Why yellow? It occurred to me. And after it occurred, I could maybe understand why—the sun, April (and the poem was written in April), flowers and spring in general, gold, preciousness. Why do people value gold? I do not need to know why, but they do. And I am there with them. . . .

Though the poem ends with "happy," I perceive in it not a frivolous but a solid and realistic human position: "maybe" is in the poem, "go by" is in the poem, "someone" is in the poem. The conditional is in the poem, all the way through it, as it is through life.

As for sound, I live in one great bell of sound when doing a poem; and I like how the syllables do-si-do along. I am not after rhyme—so limited, so mechanical. No, I want all the syllables to be in there like a school of fish, flashing, relating to other syllables in other words (even words not in this poem, of course), fluently carrying the reader by subliminal felicities all the way to the limber last line.

And I find that up to the last I was tinkering there, putting in a comma before "if you're happy," and taking it out so as to let readers coast to the end, either noticing how drastic that last phrase is, or not, thus getting just what they deserve, in the infinitely rewarding but absolutely justice-rendering world of art.

The World and "Yellow Cars"

An attitude prevalent today—and a kind of poem all but universal today—frames us into a false pair of alternatives: you can be bland, simple, innocent, a little bit dumb, and be happy; or you can be intense, profound, and smart, and realize how grim and serious life is.

The first choice people are indulgent about; the second, though, is of course the valid one, say significant people today.

But "Yellow Cars" won't accept that formulation; it, and many poems that come to me, comes from an attitude that assumes and lives in light of a different perception, one that accepts what comes, is not surprised by chance, but does not give up a tough, sustained gusto about living.

It is not my intention to defend happiness at great length here, but I do know it is possible without evasion, and that considering a poem like this one calls for early and decisive positioning: this poem embraces extremes—innocence and experience both. This poem's quirks come clear only with acceptance of its kind of being.

From the first line, a minimum experience is accepted gratefully—*some* of the cars, and they just go by—that is, they go/by. And you look at them, the yellow ones. You don't own them, and even those who do own them have a quaint wistfulness about it (but they keep on trying). Then comes a whimsically judgmental (but not assessing blame exactly) part about the mistakes and indecisiveness of people not using yellow cars. And then, a sharp last line of allegiance to the speaker's kind of life.

I mean every nuance of the poem, every time a line breaks with suspense or a roving of tentativeness, every word or syllable that acknowledges limits—"glimmering," "glances," "passing," "hope," "maybe," "care," "mistake." . . . And all hints in the language that sustain the attitude of leaning forward even while knowing the odds—I mean all of these: *some*-one, *if,* and the length, but also the terminal implication, of *lasts.* I hope the reader will get lost in a series of glimpses and retain a sense of going on from the poem into more glimpses, with a sense of there being many such, now and later, in art and in life.

Yellow is the color for many reasons—the sun, gold, light, spring flowers. But I do not make the choice by realizing the literary or worldly justifications for my choice, but by making my choice from the same set of human feelings that have given yellow its value and gold its cost.

This could be called a wistful poem, and I would not object. But the wistfulness is as tenacious as life is; the stance in the poem is powerful by being realistic and at the same time hopeful, like a healthy being, alive, vital.

The poem is about everyone, or anyone *could* be in the poem; so it says "you" look, "you" turn your head. I consciously made that wording, to be general, not just about myself. I even revised that way after starting by being the person inside the poem. I get tired of the centrality of "I" in current writing: that pronoun is often there just from habit on the writer's part—not that it happens to me, but that it happens, is usually the real point. Changes in sentence structure, so that central intentions get main-clause treatment, can help many poems. Or—changes of person, as this poem does it.

In this poem, and throughout my writing when I am in a flourishing phase, sounds make a continuous difference, in the first encounter while dreaming-writing along, and later when revising. It is not that attention is called to similar sounds (a rhyme in the first line—cars-are—is so much disguised that only looking back do you see it), but I want, and I feel, the sounds homogenized all the way through an utterance. I would have every *l* in this poem recognize every other *l.* So many skipping, intermittent touches occur to me that I despair of identifying and claiming them. Even the syncopation of a sentence, the thought-rhyme of having a series that proceeds by sinking through a sequence of predicates (don't care . . . made a mistake . . . haven't tried)—I live by these little universes.

Many congenialities of sound happen automatically when we write (when we talk, too?); they come as volunteers, and they are kept if they continue to please. I find options in successive rewritings, but I find them as the first ones came— by chance encounters and then recognition, or it seems chance.

And line breaks, too, happen along. By now, in my writing, many considerations occur to me in jotting down even first hints of a poem. I like to feel patterns—number of stresses, multi-unstressed or few-unstressed sound units, lines that carry over and make a reader reach a bit, pauses in the line that come at varying, helpful places: early in the line, middle of the line, later in the line. But I make the lines be the way they are by welcoming opportunities that come to me, not by having a pattern in mind.

Often a poem crystallizes fast, during my daily writing; that is, it flows along in a sustained burst of jotting things down. This poem was like that—one swirl of writing. But in another sense it came on very slowly, like a plant underground, becoming itself for days till it came out into full consciousness by means of my cultivating the ground on the day it found its light.

Looking back over jottings of a week or so before it happened, I find phrases and attitudes that reached out for each other and came on together, till I recognized a poem and welcomed it as mine.

Breathing on a Poem

For a Daughter Gone Away

1

When they shook the box, and poured out its chances,
you were appointed to be happy. Even in a prison
they would give you the good cell, one with warm pipes
through it. And one big dream arched over everything:
it was a play after that, and your voice found its range.
What happened reached back all the time, and the "octo,"
the "isped," and other patterns with songs in them
came to you. Once on the Yukon you found a rock
shaped like a face, and better than keeping it, you placed
it carefully looking away, so that in the morning when
it woke up you were gone.

2

You saw the neighborhood, its trees growing and houses
being, and streets lying there to be run on;
you saved up afternoons, voluptuous warm old fenders
of Cadillacs in the sun, and then the turn of your thought
northward—blends of gold on scenes by Peace River. . . .

3

It was always a show, life was—dress, manners—
and always time to walk slowly: here are the rich
who view with alarm and wonder about the world
that used to be tame (they wear good clothes, be courteous);
there are the poets and critics holding their notebooks
ready for ridicule or for the note expressing
amusement (they're not for real, they perform; if you

take offence they can say, "I was just making
some art"); and here are the perceivers of injustice; they
never have to change expression; here are the officials,
the police, the military, all trying to dissemble
their sense of the power of their uniforms. (And here
at the end is a mirror—to complete the show for ourselves.)

4

Now, running alone in winter before dawn has come
I have heard from the trees a trilling sound, an owl I
suppose, a soft, hesitant voice, a woodwind, a breathy
note. Then it is quiet again, all the way out
in that space that goes on to the end of the world. And I
   think
of beings more lonely than we are, clinging to branches or
   drifting
wherever the air moves them through the dark and cold.
I make a sound back, those times, always trying for only
my place, one moving voice touching whatever is present
or might be, even what I cannot see when it comes.

Something you are writing, after it is done, or begins to feel
close to done, you can lean over and breathe on it and try to
bring its main moves, its trajectory, into the center of your
attention.

"For a Daughter Gone Away" invites me to attain some
such perspective. Not that it strikes me as all that neat and
orderly—to me, it is a troubling, rambling poem, not a model
of unity by any means. But it gives me occasion to brood
about considerations that relate to any poem. If I breathe on
it now, I can get back to something of the feeling of shaping
any work, or so I hope.

The care—the caring—in this poem strikes me: the person
addressed is lucky, and evidence is given for that. Slowly, by
means of local, private references, the lucky person emerges—
playful, quaint, the kind of person who dwells on what has
happened, who carries along through the years many quick
allusions to family adventures—"what happened reached
back all the time."

My feeling is that all of the early part of the poem can

survive its weaknesses, even its ineptness, even its random or odd words and events, just so its direction stays steady. It is almost as if the recaller of events can be willfully obscure and relaxed: nothing can go wrong, because there is forgiveness in the person addressed and faith in the person talking. Much more important to me, in this part of the poem, is an orientation of acceptance, and that quality may even be enhanced by "blunders" or ramblings.

Because the poem does ramble, reaches onward through sections, I helped myself feel orderly by numbering the parts. In the second part the scene extends to the neighborhood; and again all is easy—it even ends with "Peace River." The reaching for places and events in this poem come about naturally: our family made many trips together, and one notable trip to Alaska, where the spaces and loneliness became part of our growing, and the names like Yukon and Peace River impressed us, became part of our common references. The keynote I feel in the early parts of the poem is security, sharing. The color is gold. The time is voluptuous.

But in part 3 certain firmer, sterner notes begin to enter. Not forcefully, but with confidence, allusions to other parts of society crowd into consciousness: other artists are coolly recognized, officials are considered and neither attacked nor admired, "perceivers of injustice" exist—they just exist—not admired, not ignored. Elliptical though this section is, I feel it as that part of the growing-up process that carefully moves toward judgment. Not until considering the poem at this remove do I feel the slightness of this portion, the audacity of its presuming to have a part in the poem, with its slim, weak, almost imperceptible touches of irony, its caution, but its refusal to skip over a needed development in such a poem as this is beginning to be.

At the end of the section one sentence attempts to ward off a whole element of risk in growing up and becoming wise: there is a mirror so that we can see ourselves under the same kind of light we have been using for other people.

By now as I breathe on this poem I feel apologetic, and for a strange, completely unanticipated reason—it is far too ambitious. Whatever justification it might have as a responsible piece of discourse depends on most tenuous hints and connections. Can it be that poetry often allows both writer and reader to swing wide on allusion and hint and loose connection, just because only by such recklessness can one reach far out for meanings, with frail helps from language? At any rate, here in the fourth section I find myself introducing my feelings and thoughts, at last, in first person. And my role in this section is to signal the pulling away of a parent, the accepting of departure, the manifesting of a continuing easy experience, taking what comes, speculating on it. . . .

I think the last part is lonely, but is not reaching out to reclaim, and is "always trying for only / my place."

Phrases like that last, they surface in poems. They are sometimes oddly inconspicuous, but it may be that the furniture of a poem, the emphasized parts, the prevalent elements, are not at all the main *motor:* a poem may provide you occasions for saying things that are so much a part of your life that you import them into even the most remote utterances. I now believe that in this poem I was blundering along through sections that offered me occasions for a few intense impulses of my own—ideas like these: you can be lucky even in prison, you can treat experience as a set of surprises on which to exercise your quirky self, you can welcome kinds of life that others might feel cheated by.

And now here at the last of my breathing on this poem I realize that in a high-handed way I used the writing of it to arrive at a statement that is spookily central to my kind of writing and to the aim of my life—the attainment of "one moving voice touching whatever is present / or might be, even what I cannot see when it comes."

Improving Your Dreams

A Course in Creative Writing

They want a wilderness with a map—
but how about errors that give a new start?—
or leaves that are edging into the light?—
or the many places a road can't find?

Maybe there's a land where you have to sing
to explain anything: you blow a little whistle
just right and the next tree you meet is itself.
(And many a tree is not there yet.)

Things come toward you when you walk.
You go along singing a song that says
where you are going becomes its own
because you start. You blow a little whistle—

And a world begins under the map.

The way you are supposed to dream is this—you study the dreams of others, especially of those who have succeeded, those whose dreams have met the test of time. You extract from successful dreams the elements that work. Then you carefully fashion dreams of your own. This way, you can be sure to have admirable dreams, ones that will appeal to the educated public.

As your technique improves, you will find your dreams accepted more and more: what doesn't work, you learn to leave out.

Of course, now and then (you won't be able to help it) some strange, untried elements will creep into your dreams—you can't be careful and responsible all the time. And of those stray flaws, a few may be good luck, and you will keep them; they are signs of some rules not yet discovered. And if you are scholarly you may save up an account of them, and later offer the account to apprentices so that they may dream properly.

Thus, over the generations, the quality of dreams will improve; a tradition will accumulate, with skills and crafts that can be passed along. Ambitious and reliable people can study about dreaming and gradually become worthy of dreaming for themselves. If they start a weak dream, one with clichés or irregularities, or if they let themselves wander into an unstructured dream that violates the best in the tradition, they can stop themselves and hold staunchly to standards.

Quality is achieved by cleaving to those standards. As one respected critic has said, "Every time you accept an unworthy dream, you are damaging the tradition of American dreaming."

IV

Glimpses of How It Is: Angles by Distinctive Interviewers

Interviews often overlap, eddying around in used-up material. But now and then an interviewer takes aim and stays distinctive.

Such aims distinguish the following: one is linked to writer-and-place, one to poetry and religion, and one to teaching and a few other things, including even accountability.

A Witness for Poetry

[When Charles Digregorio and I sat down in April and May of 1978 to do an interview for the Oregon Historical Society as part of their oral history program, we didn't know how far we would ramble. He nudged me definitely into certain topics and then got out of the way, and I cut loose.

When he wrote up the result he left his nudges out, and my spiel took on a quirky appearance. I liked the character he made out of me by his tactic, and I have not softened the zigzag effect of our talk except in two or three places where the tape recorder did not register facial expressions or gestures that helped make sense of the trajectory.]

I'd like to make everything I write have the same bite to it. Ideally for me, poems are nothing special. They are just the language without any mistakes. Of course, that is the way I would like to talk. Ideally, every letter should have the same trancelike, forward unfolding into the subject matter that a poem should have. I think poems are pieces of talk, savored and sustained. I would call them "lucky talk." A poem is a lucky piece of talk. Letters are usually addressed to someone we are sympathetic with. It can be direct. It appeals to many common experiences, usually. I think a poem is like that. . . .

In the poems I make the punctuation absolutely the most orthodox and helpful, if possible. Without it, it would be like barreling down the freeway without putting on the turn lights. Punctuation, to me, is to aid the reader in finding a way through the constructions and nuances of what is said. I know poets who have extreme ideas about punctuation. . . . They think it gets in the way. I can't help feeling that punctuation was a pretty good invention. Now and then you have to do acrobatic things because of what you are trying to do. Unless there is some reason, I would follow the Modern Language Association's style sheet for punctuation.

To me, the language is social. I don't invent it, they don't invent it; it is something that comes about between us. Usually, I don't think of the reader at all. There is a special reason that the language relates to the reader and that is, the language that I am relating to is not my invention. It is something that comes back between us. I'm still giving my primary allegiance to the language and my own experience with it, but that kind of relation is also a social relation because language on this other side impinges on the reader. If I am true to the language, I shall also be true to the reader.

At times in my thinking I take my hands off the handlebars and see what happens. In a poem I do that all the time. I let the total momentum of the experience dictate the direction the poem goes. I had a recent conversation with a student about this. He gave me two options. I could say that we respond to things because there is something in us that makes us available to these things, or we could say that "the Force" makes it happen. I opted for the first, he opted for the second; so we had a big argument.

I feel like a person with both feet on the ground. In my poems, I like to be wild, but after the poem is written and you come to me and ask about it, I would like to have both feet on the ground. As a citizen, I would like to be perfectly responsible. I think artists get into trouble with governments all the time. They have to hop across boundaries because in their creative selves they are not committed to something settled beforehand. They are committed to something that may show up ahead of them. They are creative. . . .

In the process of writing, it is awfully fast back and forth between you and the page. Even in talking, you correct yourself even before it is voiced. I suppose that is one thing that makes us nervous. When someone tells us something, we don't know how many versions they have tried out inside before the one we hear. Some people are too good at this. If I write something down, I don't feel secure about it until I have gone back and read it with the knowledge I have accumulated through having written it down the first time. It would be better to read it through the first time so you can anticipate. Revision for me is a lot like that. But in writing, it is writing the beginning without knowledge of the end. You make me realize that revision brings a greater richness to the second time through and then the third time and so on. It isn't just the beginning and the end; there are multiple things all the way through. There are dawning realizations as adjustments are made. I can imagine reading and revising an infinite number of times. For me, the language is never set like concrete; it's always like taffy. I could go over a poem I wrote years ago, but I don't. It is as if it were written by someone else; me, then. It is quite foreign, alas, to the self I am now. . . . The language changes, you change, the light changes. . . .

On the back of *Allegiances* I wrote something like, "I would like to create poems that abide in themselves. Readers may pick them up or not, as they like." This is redoing the wording, but I don't like forensic occasions myself. I do not like to feel that someone with forceful language is elbowing his way into the polling booth with me and jiggling my hand when I am voting. I want to slow it down. I want my poems not to be forensic but just to be. . . .

In a way, that is assertive. My kind of assertion is to give individuals plenty of room in which to make their own decisions. . . . To me democracy isn't the process in which any group that is loud enough or rich enough can impose ideas on another group. Democracy is a situation in which we don't try to overwhelm each other. We value what each other has to give. We all have brass bands and demonstrations, but the still small voice of reason is what I keep trying to protect in myself and cherish in others. Don't tell me what forensic speakers have forced on you. Relax, forget them. Tell me quietly, here in this room, what you really think. The speaker who forces his thoughts on you is not cherishing your thoughts. I value what you say. I'm using quiet forensics in my poems. The power of that, and its great gain over the other kind, the loud kind, is that it incorporates those silences and gives each side a time to think. The silences are important. . . .

My middle name is Edgar; that was my grandfather Stafford's name. I was born in the middle of Kansas—Hutchinson. I was drafted out of the University of Kansas at the beginning of World War II. I was a conscientious objector; so I was sent to camps in Arkansas and out in California where I met the woman who is now my wife. We settled in Oregon after I was turned loose after four years in these camps. I got a job at Lewis and Clark College in 1948. I zagged back to Kansas to pick up a master's degree, finished all the course work, and submitted a book called *Down in My Heart* as my thesis. It was a prose book about my experiences as a conscientious objector. . . .

I don't think it is hard to get a feeling for Oregon even if you weren't born and raised here. I don't feel any particular connection with a certain part of the country. It's just that wherever one lives, the arts are immediate experiences; you converge with your locale. I don't think the locale is crucial, but it is crucial that wherever you are, you converge with it. So the Northwest is spectacular for scenery, and if you are from New York you say, "Fir trees, waterfalls, yes, that is a regional poet from Oregon who writes about the land." I don't feel any special block against converging with the Oregon landscape because I was born in Kansas. It seems like they are are contrasting places, but the feeling of converging with the places is more crucial than where the place is.

I think my poetry would be different if I were somewhere else, but it is mostly because of the people, not the land. Critics are hard put to find cohesive things to say about literature; so they fasten onto spectacular words like Yakima or Walla Walla or something like that and say, "Oh yes, I can locate that person; he writes about the land." Well, Manhattan is also a place-name. It just doesn't seem like the land, but for a writer, words are the thing. To quote Alfred North Whitehead: "For a poet, a tree is a symbol for a word." . . . It is hard to find out exactly what it is that makes a piece of writing work. If I were in France, the place names would be different, but that is not crucial. What is crucial is something else, some kind of spooky, ghostly thought, emotion or a complex type of thing that goes on in poems. . . . It is a hard thing to identify; it is some kind of way you make progressions from one set of intimations to another. Something about how long you stay with one thing until you move to another, and how you move. These things are hard to talk about, but it is easy to say, "Yakima, oh yes. I know where Yakima is."

It is not so much bringing it to the surface as it is like finding that it has come to the surface. It's like discovery rather than creation, or like finding out what the language is going to do this time. This is the sort of feeling you get when doing a poem. It is not so much like telling someone something that I have already decided to tell them. It is more like watching the language do it. It's like standing by a river and seeing what comes around the bend. . . .

The language leads poets in many directions. It is not a deliberate thing, but more like where your attention is at a given time. If it goes one way, it doesn't go another. It is not so much a grim focusing as it is being distracted in a positive direction. A poem is something that starts to be something and it keeps right on being that thing. You are willing to be channeled in the direction that you start in. You lend yourself to the immediate experience that you are having. It is more important to be ready for the immediacy of experience than it is to be in some certain place when you lend yourself to the immediacy.

This sounds scary in the philosophical sense, but in the real world it doesn't work that way. The more you let yourself be distracted from where you are going, the more you are the person that you are. It's not so much like getting lost as it is like getting found.

One issue, "How the hell do you teach others to write poetry?" can be answered this way. One thing you do with others is try to encourage them, induce them and be company to them when they go ahead and follow the immediacies of experience. You tell them, "Don't be inhibited, don't be cautious, don't be correct; just go headlong into the experience."

Most people think writers have to overcome the stubbornness of the world in not recognizing what they are doing, but I don't feel that way at all. The welcoming that I got from my mother when I came home from school to tell her what happened on the playground was one of my first publications, I think. I don't think of the arts as something hitting a barrier and finally surmounting it. Rather, the arts are a kind of easing into a relation with life that makes it customary for you to respond and interact. My mother was my first editor and a very comforting and welcoming editor she was. She would ask me what happened at school that day and I would answer her; that to me was just like publication.

It would be interesting, I suppose, to ask artists when they first had something published. But to me that is not a crucial question. Earlier than that and more pervasive and important is the stance you begin to take toward the rest of the world and its relation to you. The first poem is probably somewhere in school, the teacher receives it and isn't as mad as she was the day before. That is success. So there is no certain level of success like climbing over the transom at the *Atlantic Monthly* and getting a poem in there. It's more gradual than that. It's a lot easier unless you have that artificial barrier saying, "I haven't arrived until I have published in the *Atlantic*." In that case, your life may be lost before you get anything.

I haven't reached the day yet where I say, "Today I am a Poet!" I don't want to have that kind of feeling; it's much more tentative. It's "What will happen today?" that is interesting, problematical (I started to say scary). It's a toss-up. Let's see if it is heads or tails today.

Writing poetry to me is never the same. It's like asking someone who is hungry and eating a steak, "Don't you ever get tired of eating steak?" He has to think for a minute, "Oh, yes, come to think of it, I'm doing a lot of this, but for some reason, I don't get tired." That is how I feel about writing, there are a lot of immediate things that happen. The satisfaction is a part of the activity, not part of the reward for doing the activity. That is a distinction of the arts. You have got to get the satisfaction of being harmonious with the material. That is where it is.

It is hard to support yourself, monetarily, as an artist. That is an abiding weight for a poet. It doesn't interfere with my work; in some ways, it just makes me more stubborn. "I'm going to do it anyway!" But it is a weight. I would say that ninety-five out of one hundred people I know, even the sympathetic ones, think that I am doing a pretty foolish thing.

I'm spending my life, a lot of my effort and psychic energy, on something as effervescent and frivolous as "June ... moon...." That is what people think of when they think of poetry. I don't think that is what poetry is. I don't think it is a loss, that opinion people have, but the unspoken and ever-present burden of negative judgment on certain of my activities is part of my life. I'm used to feeling different enough to say, "OK, so you don't like it!" I have done other things right along. It is not as if to be a poet you are always reciting and reading poetry. You talk, build houses, ride a bicycle....

Our son Kim and I worked on a house. We have been building a house. That is another thing. An art part of your life, I feel, is never going to be available to other people, but something obvious like building a box is available. There are a lot of people that take their opinions about art secondhand. So if you win a prize they say, "Oh, you have succeeded." That is not right, that is not it. Inside yourself you know that is irrelevant. It's somebody else's opinion. When you really accomplished something was when you did that art. When you were actually engaged in the process of writing, you were utterly alone and making decisions for yourself. While we were building the house, if a friend of mine visited and said, "That board ought to be sawed this way," I would consider it carefully. Imagine if somebody were to get into my head and say, "No, don't do it that way, do it this way!" I wouldn't pay any attention to it. What I am doing is so immediate and delicate that there is only one person involved.

When writing there is a kind of willingly lost feeling. I thought of it in many ways. There is a combination of arrogance and abjectness about being an artist. The abject part is, "Maybe it won't make any difference to anybody else, but that's OK." The arrogant part is that they don't decide what you do. Freedom in the arts is not political, it's not a superficial thing: that is the heart of it.

Human beings, like puppies, are responsive to the warmth and responsiveness in others. I have this feeling, but it is not as if the encouragement is something that you have saved up and formally voiced. It is much more homogenized with inhale, exhale, living all the time. So I am wary of the "Now, let's stop and recognize accomplishment" kind of activities. That is poison.

I think that every time you meet someone who responds to the pace and to the degree that seems to you congruent to your own pace and degree, you are responding. This happens with all kinds of people, animals, weather, whatever. I guess what I am trying to do a little dance away from is the idea that in writing one is guided by any kind of formal program that your society, friends, or teachers have. I don't think that is it. It's a much more continuous feeling of closing with the material. . . . All sorts of things have helped me. People are harmonious, so a lot of it has been people. But it hasn't been the formal approval of people. Maybe it's been the unwilling, grudging lifting of the eyebrow when they are hit by something. That is better than someone who is going to encourage you. That's poison. Encouragement signifies that someone has a program that they have already arrived at for doing something for you. I try to get away from that in my teaching. A lot of teachers become that encouragement machine. That is deadly, I would rather be envious of my students than encouraging them. . . .

Instead of trying to achieve satisfaction by fitting society's hurdles I think that the artist is the one who has chosen another kind of satisfaction that is so much interiorized that it never fails. It is like an appetite. There are times that I am not hungry, but I know I will be hungry tomorrow. I never had a dry spell about eating . . . or writing. . . .

Time entered into my thoughts immediately when I was asked to do this interview. Before coming today I thought (maybe because we are meeting in the Oregon Historical Society) that I had turned into some kind of relic and I was going to be asked things like, "How was it back in 1948?" Those were the types of questions I thought I would be asked. I didn't think it would be about the process of my own writing. . . .

It's strange to think that there might be things that we know that people that live one hundred years from now would like to know. We forget to say them. . . .

The Poet as Religious Moralist

[Not a WASP, or a WASC, I would settle for being a mixed UN-itarian; so it alerted my survival impulses to be interviewed in Provo by Clinton Larson, a professor at Brigham Young University, about religion and poetry. I did dodge about.

But the topic looms as important and is too much avoided by writers, it seems to me. So I include the central part of our interchange as a step toward more attention for this neglected, significant aspect of the writing life.]

How prominent are Christian values in your poetry?

There are not many labels on the value statements in my poetry; but my assumption is that such values are homogenized all through the lines: we acquire our values in so many little ways throughout our lives that we may become unaware of them; but a reader in my opinion could feel in the presence of such values, if alerted to search for them.

How aware are you that Christian values provide a substructure to your poems that explicitly represent a cause?

While writing, I am seldom aware of substructures; so in a way this question gets slippery to answer. But if I try to respond to the spirit of the question I would say that, on reflection, I would find such values lavishly present. And behind the explicit statements there are no doubt prevalent residues and assumptions—substructuring—from the whole wealth of Scripture-reading, church-going, and society-listening parts of my life.

Do you believe that Christian values are most effective when only implied in poetry?

Yes, I do believe that values in any direct use, any straightforward asserting, in poetry, are counterproductive for several reasons, and I would like to explain. For one thing, if you simply assert something you are likely to forget that a reader, a worthy reader, needs not just your random speaking out, but an experience of sharing the source of values, the evidence for values, the adventures inherent in the finding and maintaining of values. In short, a direct assertion is a most limited offer of experience for a worthy reader. That is one cause of my unrest about overt piling on of values.

The other main source of my unrest is that the whole validity of poetry is based on something other than just the shoveling in of content: poetry is an experience, a venturing into new encounters, an exercise of the thoughts, feelings, dreams, impulses of living human beings. To reduce life to the repeating of formulas already arrived at by others is to exclude readers from the zest and adventure essential to full living; such a reduction, no matter how well intentioned, is robbery—white-collar (or should I say white-winged?) crime.

How doctrinaire are you as a poet?

It is hard for me to conceive of anyone claiming to be doctrinaire, if that means just inertly in the presence of something already formulated: thinkers, artists are alive in the presence of experience; that is their job. But this is not to say that I feel opposed to doctrines, which are in my opinion often valuable, convenient, wise. But one has to *find out* such things, and partly by being only marginally "doctrinaire."

What religious experiences have been most meaningful to you?

Every religious experience I recall that impressed me greatly has been in the presence of influences that combined several senses—no merely verbal experience, in a church, has provided a full religious experience.

The most impressive such experience I recall was on the banks of the Cimarron River in western Kansas one mild summer evening, when sky, air, birdcalls, and the setting sun combined to expand the universe for me and to give me the feeling of being sustained, cherished, *included* somehow in a great, reverent story.

And slant, chance verbal experiences have approximated this, come to think of it—passages of Scripture, cadences in a friend's voice, habitual phrases in home conditions. . . .

Are your poems deistic or theistic?

My poems may go in any direction; and I like to think that they might catch thinkers of all kinds and make them have an adventure within the particulars of their lives. I am ready to try out extreme views and even sustained excursions of thought and feeling, as a chemist would try elements or a physicist would drop weights from a tower. If I had to try to identify the more prevalent assumptions in my harmless but reckless poems, I guess I would say they are likely to have whiffs of theism.

Do you have a firm belief about the nature of God?

My sense of the nature of God is neither firm nor infirm; it is just there: I can't perceive the degree of such sensing others have, so I can't tell whether they would think my feeling firm or infirm. Whatever it is I have—I do have something that serves me unfailingly—it is not something I can impose on others in the one direction, nor retreat from in the other. My belief is just something like where north is to a compass: I can sway; I can be confused. But north is still there.

Should poetry be used in church services?

This one is easy: church services are poetry from beginning to end; they just *are* poetry. A strange thing to me is that someone can come out of church service and ask about whether poetry is flourishing today. They have been inside singing, praying, repeating cadenced uplifting words. They are help-lessly enthralled by poetry without knowing it—that is, many of them do not know it. Religion is serious poetry—which is not to say religion cannot be lighthearted. But at its highest it turns important; and important involvement with language, use of language for significant human experiences, merges inevitably into poetry.

Is the writing of poetry an egotistical maneuver?

The writing of poetry can easily be an egotistical maneuver; maybe it often is. Maybe it almost always is. But the com-petitive exercise of any skill can be, often is, and maybe almost always becomes so: we must be alert to preserve the helpful, proper attitudes toward whatever we learn to do with fluency and grace.

In its essence, poetry, like other sustained human endeav-ors, is done best in a condition of humility and welcoming of what comes. The exploration of what the materials of life can yield to us, and the discovery of what is implicit in human experience, will work best for one who is turned outward, with trust, with courage, and with a ready yielding to what time brings into view. This practice can be the opposite of egotistical.

How can personal and communal religious insights be made to serve each other?

At first glance, or first hearing, this question sprouts barbs and puzzles. But on thinking it over I realize that to my way of thinking communal insights are arrived at by the ready and generous association of individuals; and individuals are guided and helped by the communal acquirements of their society. So—I feel easy in the presence of this apparently troublesome but actually most congenial question.

Do righteous poets have better access to inspiration?

Righteous is a troublesome word, in some of its connotations—if it means selfishly clinging to one's claims for being superior in terms of values or goodness, well, that obviously is a troublesome position to take, or to be in the presence of. . . .

But if righteous means a condition of being somehow right, or with the best perception of a society, or accepted within a community, then I would say that being righteous is helpful. *Not* being righteous, in this second sense, is a hazardous condition, a distracting condition. I feel that this issue is tangled and could be interesting, but pursuing it here would distort the proportions of the interchange—other questions may lead to convergent application that will help illuminate this one.

What are some chief trends in Western American literature?

Western American literature falls under the influence of many kaleidoscopic and disquieting changes going on around us: traditions are being buffeted by other traditions—or by the chaos resulting from uprooting and social stresses; competitions resultant from job scarcity and changing opportunities have induced a kind of gambling spirit, a short-run-calculation-only morality. Human beings flourish best where natural consequences are easy to see and not subject to maneuvers that are destructive of social trust and reliability. Our literature often follows superficial trends; and perhaps more significantly our literature becomes subject to huckstering in various guises.

In such a scene the way forward is where it always was—being trustworthy and being wisely ready to find trustworthiness in others, being steady-on with those qualities that yield abiding good for oneself and others.

How would you characterize your best poetry?

Whether my own, or that of others, I believe good poetry has early and frequent verbal events, is consistently rewarding—that is, it comes through with worthy adventures that are promised or implied in its early parts. Too many elements must combine for various kinds of "best" here; I am afraid I must turn to further questions. . . .

What advice do you have for Mormon poets and critics?

This question implies some special problems that I am not sure I believe in; but I will try to lean away from my natural assumptions of being essentially very much a part of any society that will allow me in—and I'll see if I can come up with some helpful slants.

I believe Mormon poets and critics should be neither defensive nor aggressive in relation to non-Mormon literature: be firm, brave, welcoming of what is agreeable wherever it may come from. We should all reach out for insight and company, even while maintaining whatever we do see in a special way. I think there might be a danger for artists in any group that might feel itself under the necessity of *competing*—in art there is no competing, I say.

We all share, in art. And to be worthy artists we must be ready to look around, give credit where we feel it belongs, help each other maintain that sense of community that will maximize whatever vision we are able to find and share.

I would like to close this interchange with a general statement about this writer's relation to the general topic under discussion: In my poetry, it is natural for me to assume that the values implied or explicit throughout are harmonious with Christian values, not because such is my direct purpose but because my life is permeated with those values, as a result of my upbringing and associations. Anyone in our part of the world is touched by such values (even when denying it!). Homogenized into my life are the prevalent views of those around me; I feel so easy about that prevalence that I do not have to try to maintain what is like breathing. I don't forget to breathe, and I don't forget to genuflect, in my thought, toward the whole tide of my living values. If my easy assumptions seem too casual, I hope to be vindicated by the general spirit of responses to all the questions you raise.

Facing Up to the Job

[Being a pacifist forces you into a strange kind of aggression sometimes. When Nancy Bunge was tracking down writers to find their views on writing and teaching, I found myself disagreeing—in a slant way—with some standard teaching practices. So when the two of us got going—during a blizzard in Detroit—we ranged far, and we discovered for ourselves a kind of jujitsu stance for creating, and teaching, and living.

To meander, we found, was natural to us, but our wandering discovered a harmony between us about a manner that accepts what comes in writing and in dealing with others. Even my sentences, which she left to their wavery unfolding, indicate something of that leisurely, snow-drifting day.]

When you talk about writing poetry, you usually talk about letting things happen.

It's a strong impulse of mine to put that into any such conversation about writing because I feel that it's important to let the process of writing bring about things rather than be just the writing down of things that are already brought about. Some people talk about writing as if it's penmanship: you take dictation from your psyche that has already done something. Well, I'm interested in the psyche that hasn't done something and then does something. What does it do in between? So I always try to get the people to relax enough to pay attention to the things that actually occur to them during the process of writing. Does this make any sense?

That makes sense, but how do you do it?

I do it in any way I can to keep them from feeling that they have to be on guard about what they write or that they have to have it all formulated before they begin or that there are unallowable things in dignified discourse. I'd like to go all out on this and confront as squarely as possible those who make students feel that writing is something that is done with the fully conscious, already accomplished self. I think writing is itself educational, exploratory, and worthy of trust while you're doing it. So if you think of something while you're writing, that's fine.

I still feel the weight of your question, How do you get them to do that? It's partly by creating an atmosphere of trust in the classroom. It's partly by joining them in whatever reactions we have: they sometimes feel funny about what they write; so I feel funny about it too, but I don't inhibit it. Well, there is one other thing I'd put in somewhere; I might as well put it in now: I think approval of student writers is scary to them. I keep meeting teachers who say, "Oh, yes, I'm very nice to the students. I always find something to praise." I don't like that. I would rather be neutral or the way I would be with a friend discussing something that neither of us has a fixed position on but which we are both exploring so that the friend or the student doesn't feel that they have to get that approval by doing something good again. That just extends the area of inhibition.

Oh, because they learn to write for the approval.

That's right.

Rather than for themselves.

Yes. It has the same effect as criticism, really, because even approval is the implied presence of possible criticism. So there's someone you give a lot of approval to, everybody else gets it from the other end: "They got it. Now how can I get it?" I don't see any way around that. I don't know why I have so much trouble with teachers about it.

So you just discuss what they've written and . . .

Yeah, and I would like our discourse to be about those things that don't have to do with praise or blame but have to do with more or less, or "Did you do it like this? Tell me more about why you did it like this," and not the automatic stance that is almost always imposed upon teachers of being the evaluator. I'm not evaluator; I'm participant.

Are you able to get away without grading them?

I have been able to get away without putting grades on the papers; this is a little bit different from not grading at all. Many places where I've taught, I did have to grade the students at the end of the term; but I would try to separate that function from the teaching function. The teaching part I would keep as far as possible from reminding them they are in this area where there are minefields to cross in which they might ruin their grade. So as much as possible I would postpone, dilute, avoid, play down the idea of evaluation. They would, I suppose, always know that sooner or later I'd have to grade them. But that's not part of our daily life; that's not part of the learning. That's part of what the society has imposed upon us in this institution. That's what I tell them. I think the grading procedure endangers creativity. This isn't entirely easy on them because they've gotten used to being evaluated.

Oh sure, or being told how to do it; that's much more comforting.

Either told how to do it or praised. Some people have said, "Well, Bill, you're so softhearted." No, it isn't that. It's more scary than that. But it's not scary in the sense of being haunted throughout the process of writing by the need to tailor-make what you're doing for the approval of the teacher.

Is there anything else you do?

Yes, a whole lot of things. One is I try to induce in the class-
room an atmosphere in which it is possible for reactions to
come from all directions, not just from me. I've done it in many
ways. I have a box in which I put all their papers and say, "Here
are the papers for this class. Take a look. Read it." And they
either read it in their room or check it out at the reserved book
desk; so when we talk about a paper in class, there are many
reactions. But they're the kind of reactions that come straight
across at the writers, not from high down to the writer, straight
across from the peers. And once that atmosphere is established
in the room, I can even hazard a remark myself now and then.
But mostly I don't, especially early. I learned if I start a term by
being either the one who does the evaluating or, and this is
even more insidious with the same effect, the one who summa-
rizes the discussion at the end, I'm still doing it; so I don't want
to be the terminal remarker on a paper. I would rather have a
paper slip through with *horrendous* things in it than spoil the
system of the class by saying, "The rest of you have failed to
notice that . . ." or "Let me summarize what's been said here,"
and then sort of correct everyone. Oh no. Once I can enter in
like a peer, which I really am, but the system has not admitted
that, then I try to do it.

There are many other quirks because the atmosphere in
the classroom is induced by many little things: body language,
where I sit, the time I get to class, whether I have a list of
things we have to do—all sorts of things. And I just kind of
weasel in on the class, sit in on the class, don't have any an-
nouncements about tests, or anything like that.

*You teach creative writing, but you have also taught composition and
literature.*

I would apply this to all kinds of writing. And talk, as a matter
of fact. So all the teaching for me was a long-term finessing
encounter with a room full of people who were to be wooed
over into telling me what they knew and what they didn't

know and the extent to which they knew it and the extent to which they didn't know it. And I had to go past some obstacles that had been trained into them.

A lot of obstacles.

A lot of obstacles. You know, I got a long-distance look and I feel you did too because we're thinking about those times in class in which. . . . Well, the ideal I thought of was the time when there's someone who hasn't done well in school who hands in a paper and you know it wouldn't pass one of those other courses, and you don't either praise this person for that paper or blame this person for that paper, but suddenly you're just in it together and your eyes meet and you look at certain things, and those things that they are ready to have some slight adjustment to, they do half the adjusting and you do the other half. This is where I'd like to get. I don't want to be at a height, or holding them up, but just sort of looks of recognition between us. And if you get it right, it hardly makes any difference what you say. You can say, "It's terrible, isn't it?" It's OK, for they know it's terrible in the area where we're all terrible.

Did your teaching interfere with your writing at all?

Well, I sometimes thought wistfully about those who didn't have to do any work at all. But if I was going to have to work, I didn't feel menaced by teaching, partly because of the point of view I had about writing, that I wasn't learning techniques that were going to turn me into automation as a writer, that I was continuously learning from this lowest person in the class as well as from others. They had all sorts of ideas, and I would roll my eyes as much with them as with anybody. So that's what I'm looking for, that ongoing encounter, and I thought teaching was always full of richness. Any job that tired you out so much or discouraged you so much or dulled you so much would be a hazard to other activity. But I don't quite understand how teaching, in which you have all these level encounters about books, about ideas, all these lively people, I don't see why it's a menace to associate with lively people. If you get tired of lively people, I suppose you do sometimes, well, you can always go home—and I often did. My dog would be duller.

I notice that you've had other kinds of jobs and I wonder if any of them were particularly useful or not useful to your writing?

This is sort of the obverse of the other: is teaching a hazard? Well, I say I don't know why it would be a hazard. So I turn to the other jobs and think, "Are they a special help?" Oh no, they're sort of like teaching. I remember all the conversations when I worked in the oil refinery and lots of lively people there. And forest service; I liked that. And sugar beet fields; it had its own kind of heroism. Stoop crops are frontline productive activity; it's sort of fun to do that: survive the sun, be able to make a living at something that hard. There are many others too, like construction work and electrician's helper and things like that; I would have done more things too, if I'd had the chance. The jobs are full of encounters, people; even the dead periods, hoeing weeds around the oil tank—that's a nice, repetitive, vistas-over-your-shoulder kind of job.

Was there any part of your education especially helpful to your writing? Were there any particularly valuable times, like the time you spent at Iowa? Or was it all a continuum?

My general reaction to school was good. All the way through I had all sorts of wonderful adventures. School was a good place. They had more books at school than we had at home, that makes it nice; magazines, interesting people, all sorts of good projects for us to do, and I always had a lot of gusto for school. But that forces me to respond to your other question, Were there certain times. . . . Was the time at Iowa crucial? I don't mean to demean Iowa by saying, "No, that was not crucial." For one thing, I went there pretty late in my writing; for another, I don't think any one time is crucial. I think the lucky way, the way I prefer, is a generally positive succession of encounters. And I feel that I had them: many of my teachers, many books that came my way, whole spells of reading. I smack my lips when I think of how good it was. So there are just a lot of good books; that's one thing. And you find them some places and not others. And I've always liked libraries and schools and people who were engaged in libraries and schools. Garden City Junior College: excellent! El Dorado Junior College: wonderful! University of Kansas: really great! Iowa: I loved it!

Once when you were talking about what "allegiance" means, you said, "It's like assuming good will on the part of people—I tend to do that. It's like a kind of level look at every day's experience as it comes at you and welcoming it. I feel that." When I read something like that, I see a connection between your point of view and the way you write poetry. For you, the process of writing poetry is a process of accepting and it seems to me that could easily become extended to other things.

I think what I'm trying to locate is that condition of a being who has not been distorted from the receptive, accurate encounter with experience. It's possible to overlearn fear or overlearn confidence. The conditions of life are such that they make survival depend on the organism's ability to come back level again and be ready for the conditions of life as they are on the earth. There are people who are oversensitized. The intellectual position is to be a good—let me see, what am I after, what instrument shall I use? What they use to measure earthquakes: seismograph. An individual's intellect and emotions should be like a good seismograph: sensitive enough to register what happens but strong enough not to be wrecked by the first little thing that happens. And so human beings have to occupy that position between being so steady and dumb and dull that they can't register and being so sensitive that they're wrecked by anything they register. So I just try to get into the readiness and be receptive, not stampeded, not overly trustful. I suppose we're all looking for that, but I feel the formulations that some people use disguise the necessity for avoiding both extremes. It's very easy to make powerful poems out of suffering all the time. It's all right; but that makes you a casualty.

What did you mean when you said, "So I try not to learn, disengage, because reasons block the next needed feelings"?

It links partly to this idea that for some people writing is done by fully preparing the being to come out with nothing but totally worthy utterances. And the only way to do that is not to step off the path. You've got to step off the path if you're going to explore new places; so I don't want to learn so well that I'm not learning from the encounter of now with the language. And if I had a wish to express at this point, it would be, "Save me from actually having or assuming I have the fully trained ability to write whatever is assigned to me." The person who assigned it may not have seen something that a more stupid person would enable them to see. You could both be programmed so well that nothing would ever happen to you but around and around. And that is what does happen to some writers: around and around. It's the equivalent of officialese in encounters; you get a clear, well-worked-out, and often totally irrelevant response.

In another interview, someone said that "contemporary poets often seem to be super-neurotics in a neurotic world," and you said, "You shouldn't have neuroses. You ought to be on the level."

(Laughter.) Well . . .

I'm very confused about where the cliché that artists are neurotic comes from. It seems to me that doing the kinds of things you're talking about takes a lot of courage. As you said, it's scary for your students to let go of patterns and virtually everyone I've interviewed says that's central to writing well.

Analyzing someone who does something unusual, maybe people need to have locutions to use, so they say writers are neurotic. They operate in a different way from a carpenter, but carpenters are neurotic, of course, as everybody knows. In fact, when I was getting ready to put windows in our house, the glass person said, "We people who work with glass are really neurotic." He said, "You'd better not try to do that glass yourself. You'll find out why." Well, I'll put it this way, in a positive way: I'm willing to take all sorts of tentative classifications about what we're like, we writers, but there's something I'd like to cling to and that is the essential thing that we're doing. And the essential thing we're doing is we're having enough faith in our own perceptions and decisions to make them paramount. You've just got to do it, if you're an artist. So you can say it's arrogance, or you can say it's neurotic. You can say it's humility in the face of the pattern that words want to take, you can have all sorts of myth-ings about it; I don't care what myths you have, you've got to make the decisions yourself, if you're an artist. And I would like to have students realize that as soon as possible. They come into class and the first thing they want to say to me: "How am I doing?" "What do you think?" is the rejoinder, with body language, or raised eyebrows, evasion. . . .

Once you said, "It would be too much to claim that art, the practice of it, will establish a 'good,' a serene, a superior self. No. But art will, if pursued for itself, bring into sustained realization the self most centrally yours, freed from its distortions, brought from greed or fear or ambition."

I remember that.

I don't quite understand the distinction you're making, because a self that is more centrally yours and freed from greed, fear, or ambition, sounds pretty good to me.

I probably ought to tone that down a bit, but I forgive myself for saying that partly because I was coming out on that skate from avoiding the other skate. The early part of that is I didn't want to claim that one should assume that one is creating something worthy of the ages. Not at all. So the product is expendable, but the process is precious. This is what I'd like to say. I keep meeting poets who say something like, "Well, I'm trying to do something that is worthy and lasting and beyond my lifetime," and so on. I think that's just frivolous. That's something only society decides and I don't see that it makes any difference anyway. But the process is the process of living centrally and paying attention to your own life. Surely that's worth doing. If you don't, who will? That's what living is about, and you can be distracted from living by trying to create things that will last in the terminology and the mode of society that may or may not be harmonious to your life. So I want to shrug that part off.

I think it is a big claim, and if it hadn't been an interview, probably, if I had been carefully phrasing it, I would have tried to accomplish the same thing without making such forensic claims for art. I don't want to make claims for it, but I'd like to recognize what I think I see in it and that is that real art, genuine art, comes not from hammering out something for posterity, but from making the discoveries that are yours to be made because of your unique constitution and the unique encounter you have in experience.

Are there ever any days when you don't write?

There are no days I can't write.

Are there ever any days you don't write?

There are days I don't write. For instance, I'm headlong from somewhere to somewhere else and full of distractions, and I forgive myself for those days; it's not a fetish, I think, but most days I do write.

Does that change the day at all?

Yes. It changes the day a little bit. For me, for analogy, it's sort of like jogging. If I've done my jogging it's an OK day. If I've done my writing, it's a really OK day. It's a confirming, satisfying activity to do. And it's almost devotional. Maybe that's too strong, but it's as if a day of my life deserves a little attention from life. It's my kind of attention to stop long enough, to let the evaluative, the speculative, the exploratory impulses that are native to that portion of my time be manifest in a sustained way so that I can recognize them and get sustenance from them.

One person I talked to said that you're a totally natural poet and another said that everything you write is poetry.

Is that right?

And I wonder how you got that way.

Well, "how I got those words" is the way I'd phrase it. I think that these people you talked to were generous people and I don't lightly dismiss their words. I take seriously what they said, so I try to figure out, "Now, what does this mean?" I think they're locating a kind of writing that grows out of my perception of what writing is, so I'd like to say a little bit about that.

Poems and stories and helpfully enhanced discourse of any kind, I think, are results of a trustful, undistorted entry into the language that's natural to yourself. And I suddenly glimpse the possibility of conceptualizing language as something that can be exactly congruent with your mental life. That congruency is menaced by many things: competitiveness, systematic educational distortion toward prizes, maybe even being bullied by those around you so that you just don't have the bounce that it takes to get into your own thought and language. And so I hark back to something: in our home, our parents were receptive to what we said. I never felt it necessary to distort my language or even in any serious way disguise my plans. Maybe my mother didn't want me to go fishing on Cow Creek, but we knew we were both operating in an area of general acceptance. And I think maybe that's important. So I hark back to the way I'd like to have a classroom so people can let that congruency between thought and language have its way with their discourse. I think as human beings, insofar as we cherish each other, we cherish that trust that it's all right to live your own life and even to have your own thoughts and occasionally in a mild way to express them.

Someone asked you when you found out you were a poet and you said that you wondered more about when everyone else stopped.

Yes, yes. The kind of process we are talking about is native to everyone, kids with their hopscotch and so on. Everyone. Everyone I've ever met, everyone, has what to me is the essential element of what we're talking about. They may not write what they call poems, but they make remarks that they like better than other remarks. They have that lip-smacking realization of differences in discourse. But then later they may feel, "I'm a salesman. I'm not allowed to have any lip-smacking impulses about things. I'm going to give it the way it is in the book." And so they quit, as far as I'm concerned, at least that part of their lives. So I don't think it was just a cute way to keep from saying a time, although it is hard to say a time for me; I don't know a time when I wasn't enjoying language. And I guess that's what a poet does. But I think everyone shares in this, and it's artificial to think there's a life without it. They're asking the question from the point of view that poetry is something that you have to nerve yourself to do. I don't think that's true. Not to do poetry is possible, I suppose, but it's hard and I never met anyone who didn't do it in some sense of coursing sounds, of being either delighted or discouraged about how the sentence comes out, by responding or not responding to what somebody says. You're really in a tough spot if you don't have any of those responses. And so they're asking me to enter a universe in which the values I hold dear are reversed when they ask that question. I just don't want to go into that world, so I stop.

How do you feel about workshops and the fact that there are more and more poets all the time?

I feel all right about workshops. And I don't know what they mean about more and more poets all the time. Maybe there are. In fact, I think, maybe there are; but what's this viewing-with-alarm bit? I feel that this process that's so rewarding is a right for everybody. And for those who teach workshops thinking that they are going to sift out a few gifted individuals and turn them into Miltons and Shakespeares and that the presence of other people is a problem for Miltons and Shakespeares, I say they've got it wrong. Maybe I shouldn't elaborate, but I feel strongly about that. I feel that that point of view about the desirability of only a limited number, and those only of the elite, engaged in an activity as rewarding as poetry is almost like treason of the intellectual realm or the cultural realm. I'll do it the positive way by saying, if I go to a class, I feel I'm meeting a succession of people to whom I owe individually total allegiance and commitment. I'm not looking for the ones who are going to enhance the school or my reputation or their own. That's nice, but as a teacher I believe that if there is such a thing as the lowest one in the class, they deserve the same level reception and cordiality as anybody else.

Are you saying something about school in your poem "Accountability"?

Yes, I am saying things about schools. I dream my way back into it now. I was in Wyoming, in a boom town, Gillette. We were welcomed by the teachers and the students in this town. The high school is on a hill above the town; it's a boom town with trailers and quick constructions and no perspective down the road except another boom town. I'm not trying to indict Gillette or any other town; it's just that high school students are inducted into the hall of high school with lockers, with limited library, with military recruitment posters. I saw another one this afternoon in the high school where I was, right here in Michigan. I was looking for a magazine and all I could find was military recruitment posters, and those were free and you had access to them, but the magazines you had to write out a big thing. Well, it's that sort of thing that I felt in the school. I suppose it's forced on us and so I'm not trying to indict anyone, but I suddenly felt forlorn. I thought those who talk about accountability in schools think they're talking about split infinitives or something—trivialities. I'm talking about lives, vision, hope, something plain like kindness and humility, and they'd throw their kids into a school that would teach them all about split infinitives and send them straight over to drop bombs on someone. Is that accountability?

Accountability

Cold nights outside the taverns in Wyoming,
pickups and big semi's lounge idling, letting their
haunches twitch now and then in gusts of powder snow,
their owners inside for hours, forgetting as well
as they can the miles, the circling plains, the still town
that connects to nothing but cold and space and a few
stray ribbons of pavement, icy guides to nothing
but bigger towns and other taverns that glitter and wait:
Denver, Cheyenne.

Hibernating in the library of the school on the hill
a few pieces by Thomas Aquinas or Saint Teresa
and the fragmentary explorations of people like Alfred
North Whitehead crouch and wait amid research folders
on energy and military recruitment posters glimpsed
by the hard stars. The school bus by the door, a yellow
mound, clangs open and shut as the wind finds a loose
door and worries it all night, letting the hollow
students count off and break up and blow away
over the frozen ground.

V

Teaching and Writing
and Performing

A Priest of the Imagination

["A Priest of the Imagination" makes a claim for creative writing and makes it, I am afraid, with some extra swagger. But the occasion called forth the swagger. My job was to help represent creative writing programs at a meeting for people who head college English departments, and I wanted to point up distinctions in approach and at the same time dare to make the creative way pertinent in all writing courses.

Maybe the swagger here is not excessive after all, for many writing courses should be much different. I wanted to say, "Teachers, wake up."]

Lit Instructor

Day after day up there beating my wings
with all of the softness truth requires
I feel them shrug whenever I pause:
they class my voice among tentative things,

And they credit fact, force, battering.
I dance my way toward that family of knowing,
embracing stray error as a long-lost boy
and bringing him home with my fluttering.

Every quick feather asserts a just claim;
it bites like a saw into white pine.
I communicate right, but explain to the dean—
well, Right has a long and intricate name.

And the saying of it is a lonely thing.

Even before we settle down at class time on that first day in a writing course, my tentative, artful job begins.

Preferably, I won't be carrying books or outlines or guides of any kind: a professor, one of the samurai in action, I drift in, turn to the students, and—just as a writer does—I accept what I have. In the immediacy of encounter I start to learn the moves to make.

They know it's a class. They know which class. If I wait, be easy in talk—on anything for a few minutes—they will tell me. Their voices will turn on in that room, and I will yield to their sayings. Yes, it is a course in writing. Yes, the bookstore has stocked certain materials to help—and, that's right, that's one of the books there in your hand.

In a slow evasive way, I let the term ease into being—evasive, because . . . because this course is different; and I am going to balance here and let them find out how different it is.

This difference is not something I proclaim; in fact, I try to play it down. Maybe an example will help. Once I drifted into class and was lucky enough not be be recognized—they assumed I was a visitor because I sat down in the back of the room and looked around awhile. It was delicious to hear them talk, but I finally got up and walked to the front and let them decide I must be the teacher. We changed the chairs first—around in a circle. A helpful girl beside me then asked if the book she had—a paperback essays of Montaigne—would be our first reading, for background in writing. I began to act uncomfortable.

Well, I had thought of that, and chronologically it was the earliest writing in our set of texts. But now I was wondering. I rambled into apologies—maybe they shouldn't read Montaigne. He was a skeptic, and not just a little bit skeptical, the way some of us might consider ourselves, but so corrosive that you'd never be the same if you even sampled him. I offered to side with anyone who decided not to dip into Montaigne. If their parents might not approve, I said, I would understand.

I clowned this a bit, but let something serious be apparent, too. The helpful girl was surprised. I saw her take out a little notebook and begin to write. By the time our first meeting ended she was ready for me:

"Mr. Stafford, I hope you won't take this wrong, but . . ."

I took the little pages she held out. I indicated a readiness to read them, but she apologized some more.

"Please don't think I am blaming you."

I entered into the mood and said I would take the paper with me to my office and sit down and be ready for whatever it said.

"OK."

At the office I read it. A miserable scrap of paper, written on both sides, with no margin, no heading. It said something like: "Mr. Stafford, why do you say you fear Montaigne? Is it because your faith is so weak? . . ." It went on to lecture me about being braver, being ready for new things. And it began to dawn on me that a wonderful thing had happened.

The term had begun. The first theme had been written. And the student didn't even know it. Rich! Just what I had always hoped for—to be informed by the students, not to be a monument waiting for their efforts, but to be a participant in communication.

When I went to the class the next time, I took the paper with me. But I didn't give it back. I held it and stared awhile and looked at the writer. I didn't say good or bad; and I didn't agree with her, or disagree. I considered. I told her I'd think some more about it, that it was a complicated issue.

That student kept on telling me things, through her whole college time. One of the triumphs of my teaching career.

Now—this feeling in the classroom is crucial. If I start in the stance of being the judge, the advocate of culture, the parental figure, I will have a hard time reaching into the spontaneous thoughts and feelings of the group. At almost any cost, I must avoid that stance. And I will do extreme things to achieve what I want in the class.

"How much do we have to write?" someone may ask. I am puzzled by such a question and allow myself to appear so. If I am lucky enough, some brash student will opt for writing very little, and I can drop into position one: being solicitous instead of firm. For that option is so insane—to take a class and then try not to do it. I let myself be stunned by so odd an idea.

But I do not contend against this manifestly confused (and valuable to me) student.

"What if my work isn't good enough?" That will be impossible: in this class, by definition, what you can do is all right. Here, you start where you are and go somewhere.

"How can I tell when I am doing all right?" On that I can't help: such an assessment is at the heart of what you are learning to do for yourself.

All through this beginning minuet I am letting them become aware of a process unusual in their experience. I am confident, but unexpected; for this class does have something new to offer. These students are going to find out that I am the doctor, but they must tell me where it hurts before I can prescribe. Further, the medicine is not something they choose to have or are used to having, but something so specific each time that they won't be able to reach for it from that open shelf of praise, blame, rules. No. It won't be that.

"Then what are we doing?" I can hear students (and most teachers) exclaim. No praise? No blame? But will I even read what they write? With some measure of deliberation I promise to. Will I understand it? Yes. Will I mark mistakes? No. Well, will I put a grade on it? Not if I can help it. But will I myself be forming an opinion of the effectiveness of their writing? Yes.

Puzzlement. Maybe dismay. Maybe anger. How will they learn then? Ah.

Now we are getting somewhere. There are many, many things to do, but I let them struggle into the realization that they will not be the usual things—and that my pressing for certain standards of writing is definitely not one of them.

This interval of adjusting to a new kind of class is so entertaining to me that I have to guard against enjoying it so much that I prolong it just for the experience. My justifications do depend on certain principles and assumptions, and I am ready to advert to these; but first an example of practical application may clarify how the actual class sessions can go.

One such move is this. I take a box to class, an envelope box maybe—something that can hold papers flat, and be easy to carry. I put the box before them and call it the box and do some of my bustling around that they are now used to. "The box? What's it for? My idea is to use this container for everything anyone writes—this way, we can all have access to the material coming out of the class." (I am assuming that of course everyone will be interested, but I don't assert so.) Where will the box be? I think I'll put it at the reserve book desk in the library; that way, anyone can ask for it and read it over.

I promise to read the box once a week myself. And I might put something in—though of course I am busy. . . .

At no time have I mentioned who should put something into the box, or how often, or how long the papers should be. Such issues do come forth, as the class puzzles over this odd project. (The "good" students are especially given to wondering aloud how much they are expected to do—I treat such concerns lightly.) But I do have a rule—please don't leave what you put into the box in there for more than two weeks. Otherwise, the box will get too full, and when a reader goes through it there will be a clutter of things already read.

I suggest that students mark each other's papers if they like—be helpful.

If you have done this maneuver right, and in a class not spoiled by too much guidance and hovering, the box will fill up, I have found. And many advantages appear. One is that anyone in class can go and find out how others are doing, any time. This realization has many wholesome effects.

I bring the box to class each time, and cluck over it and shake my head, and shuffle things around. We read from it, each author by turns. The students have plenty of chances to react, and I listen and squirm or show envy or quick impulses at specific locations during the reading. But I never assess a whole paper or judge a person. Puzzlement in places, yes. Curiosity about further information, yes. Quirky, alive reactions, any time.

These reactions in class are the only kind I permit myself when reading through the box, too. I think of any marks as "Kilroy was here" remarks. I want the students to know I am with them, that I do have reactions. But my reactions are only those that a friend would have during a conversation. You may have to say, "How's that again?" Or, "Is that the theater we both know about on Sixth?" But you would never say to your friends, "Excellent style!" Or, "Why don't you learn standard English?" In such an atmosphere, friendship—and communication—would wither. I'll have none of it, none of that withering attitude.

Now. Space. What is back of this evasive way of doing a writing class?

One assumption is to me most important: my allegiance is to the students in the class, to each student—equally. Through all the moves as we start, I keep track of this principle; it will make a few things more difficult at the start; but it will make everything easier later.

Consider for a minute. Suppose I feel the responsibility to meet certain standards. Think of it seriously: the student becomes an element in a situation that may strain our encounter. A standard may be scary to the student; it will be presented so. But an increment in one's own life? That is easy. And my job is with increments, entirely so. The student should not worry about standards. I won't. And I will never try to make the student either complacent or panicked about external obligation. Never. That kind of measuring is not what art, what writing, is about.

Bosses may do what they will, later. Administrators may have to be accountable in their way. My way to be accountable is related directly, simply, honestly, nonthreateningly (and nonpraisingly) to my individual student. For that student, my role is to be a priest of the imagination. We share encounters, and my job is to try that no soul be lost, ever.

Let's stop for a minute, about praise. One of the burdens I feel when I talk about this way of teaching is that people assume I am just being sentimental, or kind, or cowardly. Even some who want to be friendly about the nonjudgmental way startle me with their assumptions, as they proclaim that they always "look for good things to say." I shiver at this.

The stance of the teacher who praises is in some ways as scary as the teacher who blames. Praise given now may be withheld then. And the student who is praised becomes a coercive factor to all other students. Further—how about it?—praise used as motivation is not the gold standard. Students know it. It must haunt their lives.

Once I was at a conference for teaching Indians, Eskimos, and Aleuts. Teachers from special schools were there, and students. I presented my "no praise-no blame" view and was taken to task by veteran teachers in Indian schools. One of them said emphatically that Native American students are so insecure they need lavish praise all the time. (Students were sitting in the back of the room.)

It happened that I was staying in a dorm with the students, and in conversation that evening I raised my question: Do we really have to have all that laying on of praise? One of the students spoke for the group: "It gets heavy, man."

So, when a student speaks or writes I lean forward, entering the language from my side, understanding; for that is my job. Am I a good reader? Yes, I am. A good listener? Yes. That is my job. Am I disappointed or angry? It might happen so, but that is not my job. Whatever society may do, it is outside our relationship; we are together, associating toward any little next increment and welcoming it, being artists together.

Space. That is how I face a writing class. The assumptions behind the moves help me stay oriented, as each encounter is different, but each is available to discoveries related to the goals and assumptions. Because the process is indeterminate in its details, it may seem that I am evading later problems in my account of how to begin. Let me affirm several discoveries and then just abide judgment.

The way works. I never feel shaky about it. Even students who at first are surprised or affronted come around. For one thing, the better ones, the more alert ones, are there in every class to help. They catch on and thrive.

The class sustains you. You share papers; you look consideringly at each other. You never need—the teacher never needs—to praise or blame. All issues are particulars. Every student is totally responsible for individual writing.

In practice, students will begin to follow certain leads in class. Some students will become helpers. I allow myself to be perceived as impressed, sometimes, but not as a patronizing welcomer to someone who is meeting standards. My attitude is more likely to appear as envy, or relief. I can shiver, but I can't praise. Praise what? Who knows which increment is crucial for the individual? I am a confessor, a priest. Not a judge. And about those sins, those flounderings along in language—I practice them myself.

The Door Called Poetry

[*Learning* magazine, for teachers in grade schools, asked me to write about teaching from a poet's point of view. I felt a surge of ambition—to help reduce that distance pupils are induced to feel between themselves and "literature." I reduced it by starting with a slight piece about first grade at the beginning and an actual transcript from a preschooler at the end; but my article was identified as "Exploring the Wild, Surprising World of Poetry."]

First Grade

In the play Amy didn't want to be
anybody; so she managed the curtain.
Sharon wanted to be Amy. But Sam
wouldn't let anybody be anybody else—
he said it was wrong. "All right," Steve said,
"I'll be me, but I don't like it."
So Amy was Amy, and we didn't have the play.
And Sharon cried.

Is this poetry? In my view, yes. In my view, though, poetry, like breathing, happens all the time, but—like breathing—at its best it should get little attention.

In the classroom, any time anyone says anything or jots down anything, some of what is said or written is luckier than the rest—and poetry is language with a little luck in it.

Those lucky places—everyone stumbles upon them; they are homogenized into our lives. And in class I try to recognize what comes at me, not to commend or admire, and not even—usually not even—to mention it, but simply to feel it myself. The signals I give off when someone says or writes something that lucks into poetry will come naturally—in my eyes, in the way I lean forward, maybe even in my sudden look of envy.

It is that immediate response to language that counts. Sometimes it seems to me the best equipment for being a teacher of talking and writing and reading—of communication—would be a wonderful rubber face that would register every nuance; my role would not be that of approving or disapproving, but simply (and it's not simple) that of realizing, realizing everything, all those amazing, miraculous connections that language and the mind make with each other.

When we are with children we are constantly in the presence of these sparks. To do poetry is to read or speak or write or listen with a readiness for the surprises, the bonuses that come on the individual wavelength of any human being. To organize the response, to try to coerce it so that it will be correct or approved in any way is to violate the nature of what poetry is. And that is why—though I am a poet myself, and a teacher, and a student—I get very jumpy in the presence of many poetry lessons.

So—in the classroom I wouldn't even use the word poetry if I could help it. I would try to keep students from knowing how educators have codified and classified and labelized the approaches to this shimmering and unexpected field full of goodies.

If an alert student would look at a page of poetry and say it is fat or skinny, I would feel better than if the student said it was iambic hexameter.

OK—I know we have some disagreements about this. And of course many authorities, some of them awesome, would clobber me. Still, let me sing my song, for there is one to be sung about the sidling approach in the classroom.

The turn from the authority way in poetry came to me vividly when a student was reading her theme in class not long ago. The others began to talk about it, and I listened awhile (my best tactic) and then had to ask, "Megan, wasn't there something strange in the way you moved along in that first part?"

"Well, you see," she said, "I wrote this first as a poem, and then I made it an essay." Then she went back to talking to the others, while I brooded about what she had said.

I know this student well, so I dared interrupt again: "Do you very often do that?"

She briefly turned to me and said, "Oh, yes. I usually write an essay or a story first as a poem." And she went back to the more important issues she was discussing with the other students.

Naturally I had to interrupt one more time. "Why?"

She was patient with me. "Writing a poem is more direct and simple and easy. I can put down things as they come to me, and I like to let myself ramble along the way I feel while I am writing."

It was an ordinary afternoon, but I permitted myself to lean back and savor a historic moment, a moment like that when a monk in the Dark Ages first read a page without moving his lips. I had been present when a lucky young person let me glimpse a new generation's easiness with one of the arts. The occasion was all the more satisfying for my having come out of my own Dark Ages when we students were so instructed in poetry that we were ready for the literature of greeting cards: if you had a rhyme, you had a poem.

With this new class, I was meeting students who had found the freedom and opportunity there is in language: letting it carry you as you explore forward along the line that develops where your own sensibility touches a theme.

That line cannot be predicted, if you are to take advantage of what the language begins to offer the ready talker or writer. Our students, if we give them our company, our responding presence during their questing (the rubber face again), may be induced to accept their own discoveries and to feel the satisfaction of converging with those resonating helps in language.

Let's face it, though—poetry will always be a wild animal.

There is something about it that won't yield to ordinary learning. When a poem catches you, it overwhelms, it surprises, it shakes you up. And often you can't provide any usual explanation for its power.

For all of us in our careful role as educators, there is something humbling in the presence of the arts. There is no use thinking hard work and application and responsibility will capture poetry. It is something different. It cannot live in the atmosphere of competition, politics, business, advertising. Successful people cannot find poems. For you must kneel down and explore for them. They seep into the world all the time and lodge in odd corners almost anywhere, in your talk, in the conversation around you. They can be terribly irresponsible.

In a class I visited once, the teacher had copied for the students on the board in front a "poem for the day," a pleasant verse by a successful someone who affirmed feeling lonely and liking to think about warm little animals. But on the board in back—where the teacher looked—was this:

> When I have fears that I may cease to be
> Before my pen has glean'd my teeming brain,
> Before high-piled books, in charact'ry,
> Hold like rich garners the full-ripen'd grain;
> When I behold, upon the night's starr'd face,
> Huge cloudy symbols of a high romance,
> And think that I may never live to trace
> Their shadows, with the magic hand of chance;
> And when I feel, fair creature of an hour,
> That I shall never look upon thee more,
> Never have relish in the faery power
> Of unreflecting love!—then on the shore
> Of the wide world I stand alone, and think
> Till Love and Fame to nothingness do sink.

So—there is a strangeness in our work when we deal with poetry. It ranges from high to low. We can find it in Keats, and we can find it, as I did, in the words of a preschooler telling his mother about his day:

This has been an awful good day.
First, I found a snake
then an old rotten dried-up mouse
then a baby dead mole
and then an old part of a gun.

The snake will probably get away.
A cat will eat the dried-up mouse.
The baby dead mole's mother will take
him to her nest.
But I'll keep the old part of a gun.

Making Best Use of a Workshop

A workshop? It may be as simple as a day or so of meeting with friends to talk about each other's writing. Or it may be a week or so with teachers of writing, or a term in a school, or even a whole curriculum leading to a degree. Whatever—its main ingredient is meetings among people with common interests and with know-how or insight to share.

It sounds straightforward and positive, but such apparently sociable and worthy gatherings rouse strong feelings for or against. Workshops are denounced for misleading the inexperienced, for pretending to offer quick entry to a career that really depends on native ability or at least on long and lonely struggle to attain a knack that cannot be taught or learned in sessions with others. And workshops are denounced as schemes for "experts" who cynically meet—and as minimally as possible—with dupes who put out their money for something not available: "teachers" engaging in white-collar crime.

To indict workshops for such abuses can obscure what they can be and often are. How can you engage with other writers and gain what they have for you without succumbing to the dangers in such conferring?

Start with teachers: if you believe your function is just to sort out abilities and to encourage talents you find while discouraging others, then you will find many who want just that in a workshop. They will ask for it; they will ask whether their writings are any good. And you can tell them: you stand at the gate and admit the worthy. In that role you are not a teacher, of course; and you should make clear what you are doing.

And if you are a student wanting to know just whether

your writing is any good, you may find that out fast. And if you believe the verdict, you may cut your losses and engage yourself elsewhere.

But if you are a teacher, if you can help induce the practices and satisfactions that derive from engaging with language, no matter the student and at whatever level of competency, then you can enter into that sustained interaction that is the heart of a workshop. Then you are being a teacher, not just a judge, not just an editor, not just a guardian of the flame.

And if you are a student you may find in yourself a continuing way of life that is enriched by the practice of art. What you might have identified as your goal—publication, fame, praise—you may discover to be incidental to satisfactions that come with working out by means of the materials of art the values and needs of your central being. For you, a workshop can help; in it you deepen your understanding and feelings about your own and others' writings (and talk, and gestures, and manners). You find that a workshop is not just a test; it is a concentrated encounter with experiences that relate to what you have chosen to do.

With such in mind, how can you best use your time in that setting? Teacher or student, what can you anticipate?

Well, each person's gain depends largely on what others contribute: interchange is the life of a workshop. A session where people freeze up—from fear, from competition—is impoverished. A workshop flourishes when counsel flows around. A few minutes as a workshop begins can encourage this system. Comments that can't get into utterance can be jotted down and passed along to the writer whose work is under discussion.

Think about which work of yours you should submit. Should it be your best? Maybe your most troubling? Maybe your most representative? Even to consider this point may help alert yourself and others to what actually happens when the group meets. It is not always the "best" manuscript that sparks the most learning. And what is this "best"?

What kind of reactions, and notes, would you like to receive? Usually the quick responses will be about details of the text in hand; but there may be related topics, expansions on what is present, insights suggested by what is on the page. Some ideas that surface can lead to portable principles to keep in mind throughout your later creating. The group may be able to formulate their discoveries for guidance in later composition: what is said about one text can help all those who participate, not just the one who wrote what is under discussion.

Usually, "corrections" will predominate. "You shouldn't do that." "Never start a poem like. . . ." But not just corrections, and not just approvals are in order. There will be glimmerings, confirmings, alternatives, developments from what is already present. If an easy atmosphere has grown up, these enlargings of attention will be welcomed. At such times a discussion takes off. Perspectives around the circle will open more learning than any one person could have anticipated.

Sometimes the group will cover such a range of discoveries that what accumulates is like a checklist for a pilot before take-off—oil pressure, controls at ready, runway clear. . . . When writers disperse for home, there will be habits for the final careful grooming before a poem goes into the world. A good workshop will uncover—or remind about—many kinds of tuning that get built into the writer's procedure: choice of persona, line breaks at optimum, language tuned, first-draft scaffolding taken down. . . .

But hovering over all workshop interchanges is an opportunity for something more important than any adjustment, than any guiding toward publication, than anything to do with craft. Hardly anyone talks directly about this larger opportunity, and it usually edges into consciousness only at late, lucky sessions when many influences combine to help. Short of such a harmony session, here are a few questions to approach this lesson beyond craft:

When we look at someone's manuscript in a workshop are we trying to correct it so as to make it the best possible piece of literature? (Please do not be hasty here—there are other questions.)

Are we trying to make the manuscript before us change so as to become the most likely to achieve publication? Please note that this question suggests significantly different endeavors from the first.

Are we allowing ourselves merely to adjust a manuscript toward being less vulnerable to criticism? This limited endeavor—we may be reduced to it as a result of the pressures and habits indulged in a workshop—could distract from an endeavor much more satisfying.

The more satisfying goal involves embracing a different attitude toward writing and life. Workshops thrive, even when they flounder, even when sabotaged by cynics who teach in them while indulging their scorn, because the practice of writing holds before every individual a constant promise: perseverance in art allows repeated bonuses when the material of the art finds itself merging for delicious intervals with the relevant experience of a unique life brought, as if in a trance, as if guided by currents deeper than consciousness, into individual realization.

No editor, or teacher, or market, can impose a judgment so significant as the attaining of this harmony by which the practicing artist lives.

A workshop can help in the attainment of this combination of sociability and freedom. From such a workshop a writer can depart ready for what comes.

Leaving a Writers' Conference

When we all leave here tomorrow
some will be glad, some sorry.
It will be homeward for some,
but for some it will be long
till anything lasts again.

Two weeks, a week, a day—
and you turn around and it's gone.
But it's part of the contract, you know.
I don't care, do you?

Listen—if it was OK
this time, the world can surprise us
again. And we're all going somewhere
—nobody knows how far—
circling what's never quite said.
I say it's all right. So long.

Performing and Poetry

[Gail Miller set up this interview in order to explore the links between writing poetry and the speaking of it. Her guidance is evident from the first, and she stayed alert to that primary aim, bringing us back again and again to considering sound, the feeling of action, the oral aspect of language.

Most poets get involved in readings, and as we all know, many slight the needs of the audience. Gail Miller helped me realize the importance of considering how to present a poem—and also the lurking importance of our physical guides while we write, our subtle reliance on throat and muscles in language.]

I've felt that writing poetry is a kind of physical response for you, is that true?

Yes. Actually, you enhance my feeling about this by your phrasing of it. You made me go into all sorts of quick speculations in my mind that maybe language, not just poetry, but language in general, leads us to participate in those things that are back of language; that is, we have a kind of emblem experience within ourselves when we participate in the language either reading it or hearing it. Whatever happens to the hearer or the reader is from the whole experience, and that may come from body language, it may come from all sorts of sympathies or antipathies about the voice, and the pace of it, and from many chance collisions with parts of language that we writers or speakers can't, of course, fully anticipate. So there are many chance factors that enter into any person's experience with language.

When you were teaching did you speak very much about poetry as a physical experience?

I slide into this by saying that all through the last part of my teaching, say the last ten or twelve years, I was increasingly persuaded that what happened in the classroom depended on things that I used to ignore. So that my way of going to the first session of a class became pretty stealthy. I used to think, "What can I say, what can I tell them this first session in order to make the term go right?" And I now realize, it wasn't what I was telling them, it was some other things. It was how I came in, it was how long a time I gave them to respond to each thing or to myself. It's some kind of participation with them, or what began to develop in the class. So, not just as a poet, but as a teacher, I was a total participant if I could be in what was happening. So I think I found myself edging into your area of interest as a teacher.

Did you or your students do much in the way of reading or performing poems aloud?

Part of my act was not to be the expert performer of poems. I might have been, but I tried to make it casual and to accommodate poetry to their everyday experience of the language. So I minimized the distance between them and the poem if I could. A very blunt, open way was not to talk about this poem as poetry, but to participate with them in being in the presence of what really was a poem, whether I called it that or not.

I like that word "presence" in one of your poems, "Song Now." I got the feeling you were saying that what was really special about poetry or art or music was the fact that it forced you to be in the present; that you couldn't fall into the past or the future. Is that what you meant?

Yes. It interests me that you would fasten onto that poem. I don't think anyone else has ever mentioned that poem to me. But I remember how it goes and the "is" is part of it. And I remember the feeling at the end of the poem, "it can save this place."

Yes, that's what I felt you were saying was really the saving grace of poetry, that demand for presence.

We come together pretty easily here.

You have said that writing a poem was like running fast and scraping elbows and knees in an exhilarating and very unpredictable process. Does that sensation come to you at the very beginning of writing a poem or does it gather momentum as you go?

I can get at this I think by saying that the beginning for me, can be anything, really, minimum things, nothing. And then the excitement, the process, begins to go. It picks up momentum because the second thing relates to the first thing, and the third to the first two, and the fourth to the first three and so on, and it becomes a cumulative kind of experience. And I think about the beginning—even this morning when I got up and began to write, I found myself a luxurious place lying down on the couch in the living room, and began to feel good about writing. And there's a strange thing—someone once charged me with being too optimistic and I said, "Well, maybe my poems are optimistic because I write lying down and it feels good." It's pleasant. It's hard to feel pessimistic when I'm just cozily there on the couch. So I think this links to the kind of issue you were raising.

I once read a writer who said, "This poet I know happens to be a fly fisherman, it's one of his favorite sports. I feel that I perceive in his poems that bodily activity working its way into the rhythm of the poem: that spun-out line and the feeling of an arc to the line." Does that seem farfetched to you?

That area one enters in trying to perceive someone else's process is a murky one; so there's no way for me to be sure how accurate someone would be in linking a person's writing to something as local and definite as fly-fishing. But the idea of linking the totality of one's actions and experiences in life with certain identifiable physical processes, that I do believe, yes. I do understand.

109

Do you have any particular physical activities that you think might work their way into your poems?

Yes, and I think this would be damaging to me in many people's minds, but one of the things I think of is this—mostly I like prose-y things. I like syncopated rhythms, you know, broken rhythms, things that start and stop, vagrant impulses, rather than marching rhythms. So that the surprise of action, say walking across country and coming upon things that are unexpected. . .

Your poems do have a lot of walking in them.

Yes, that would be typical of my way of going. It would not have planning ahead of time, but arriving with surprise, but I hope with grace, at what emerges as one goes along. So people who would theorize about writing, or in fact who would write with a foreordained rhythm, or feel satisfaction about fitting their process into something already established, would make me nervous. I may do that, but I'm just signifying that it wouldn't be my way of perceiving myself. In fact, I do know that most things I write have regularities; but those regularities usually reach people by way of surprise.

And they reach you by way of surprise, too?

They do.

In a dialogue you had with Richard Hugo, he was talking about the primacy of sound for both of you in writing poetry. He said that "truth has to conform to music even if it doesn't." Do you agree with that?

I understand that, in terms of the context we are talking about, in terms of literature. That's right because that's what literature is about; what truth is about I don't know. But what felt truth is I know a lot about; that's what literature's about: the feeling of it. My assumption is that we human beings don't arrive at truth anyway. It's not something we have control over at all. But our satisfactions are within our control; those things we do manage. And I think Hugo was talking about that feeling that one gets from literature, how it is related to music, to sound. By the way, Hugo was capable of casting a long cast for concepts to be helpful. And I was delighted again and again with his farfetched notions.

Someone asked if you revised, and you said, "I revise outward, I get the feeling that there's got to be more." When you're revising is it the music that's often guiding you?

I think it is. I almost said, "I'm afraid it is," because there's a part of me that feels that discourse should be entirely rational, should have to do with concepts, with logic, with certifiable, proven progressions. My progressions are perhaps provable after the fact, but I don't progress because I think they're going to be provable. I progress by hunches and echoes. Sometimes when I change (I started to say when I revise, whichever you like), when I'm juggling things that I've written and I've juggled a word out, I'm likely to juggle in a word that relates by sound to the word that's gone out. I feel guilty about this because it sounds as if I'm willing to distort everything else in the poem for the chance that another word with a similar sound can go in here; but that's what I do. I've talked to other writers about that. I said, "Sometimes when you finish a poem and you've revised it, do you hear a little faint echo of what you've taken out?" And they say yes. And I do too.

I noticed you like to link some of the end rhymes together.

For me the language rhymes; but also any sounds anywhere in the poem are never at rest; those sounds remain hanging in the air, echoing or contrasting or sustaining one's momentum. So even connections that are not perceptible to a reader or a hearer are hovering in the air for me in a poem. That is, for the writer all sounds in a poem influence each other.

I noticed that you did that in "The Unnational Monument Along the Canadian Border." There was that linkage of sound and feeling.

And you see those if they are in crucial places, but you proba-
bly don't see them if they're not; but I feel them even if
they're not in crucial places. I guess that's what I'm saying.
Subliminally they influence you. A "you" being any critic, or
anyone who's analyzing the work. There will be parts of that
work that you will never drag into attention, but they're still
working on you. That's my faith.

*I think that's what happens with that very bodily response; you feel it
intuitively.*

Oh yes. The whole thing is alive. It's not just the parts that the
critic thinks to call attention to. In fact, I just thought of this:
it would be possible to call attention to things in such a way as
to distract from the most influential things that are happen-
ing. That is, you would take a person's attention toward the
loud, obvious, identifiable linkages, thus reducing the insid-
ious influence in the parts not called attention to.

*Someone once asked you if you had a theory about line breaks, and you
said, "Yes, I do, it's what opportunities do I get, what opportunities do
I give up by breaking the line at any particular point on the page."
You talked about the feeling of sometimes getting an acrobatic swing-
ing from line to line. And I thought, "There again is that physical
response." I wondered if there were other things, other structures,
aspects of poetry where you feel those same kinds of opportunities.
Maybe the tensions, the resistances?*

Yes, I think there are many, and I don't feel confident in
being at all adequate in bringing these up in the right se-
quence or being exhaustive. But for instance, there would be
a certain kind of pleasure (and I rub my fingers together), a
certain kind of tactile experience about language that would
have to do with no more than maybe alternation of short
sentences and long sentences. Or some kind of slow rolling
rhythm of dependent elements being ahead of what they de-
pend on and then being after what they depend on. And
there would be such things as staccato sections in relation to

more slow rhythm sections. These things are only in a rudimentary way identified in the terminology that's used when people talk about poetic forms. There's a lot more to the language than what we have ever labeled, and that's the glory of it. An image comes to me; it's as if I imagine maybe there's someone who spins yarn. And as they spin, they let the yarn go through their fingers. I'm making this up, but a person who wasn't used to this would just feel that yes, a string is going through my fingers. A person who is used to spinning would feel the little patterns that are going through; they would feel it's more or less adequate as it goes and they would adjust as they went. I think that writers are like those good at spinning yarn; they can feel the material go by, the language, all sorts of little things going through the syllables and their relations, the pace of things. Sometimes when I hear someone read something I know well, either someone else's or my own, I feel a whole orchestration of reactions that has to do with the pace with which they hit certain parts or hesitations that they either ought to have or oughtn't to have; you know, things like that. So I guess I'm rambling too much, but you opened a gate that made me think, "Oh, yes, there are an infinite number of variations in the language as it goes along."

Have you heard any other people perform your poetry? Do you have a style of performance that you prefer in terms of your own work?

I haven't many experiences of this, but a few times, yes. For instance, there's a record that I think the National Council of Teachers of English put out where someone read a poem of mine, "Fifteen." And I was skeptical when I saw it was on the record. I thought, "I'll listen to this and see what happens." I thought it was great! I thought this person really waltzed through it right. And I was curious: how did this person happen to do it? And one of my theories was, well, I wrote it right. My punctuation was right, my line breaks gave the right signals, but I don't know if that's true or not. At any rate, I felt great approval, enthusiasm, and envy at how that person read it.

How many poetry readings do you do a year?

I do a lot of poetry readings. A number of years ago I counted from the calendar after the year was over and I'd gone to thirty-five or so different campuses to read. So that's thirty-five hours of reading. And it's an easy thing for me to do, reading. I don't want to be addicted to it; I'm not addicted to it. I can very easily do without those readings. On the other hand, I don't dread them. I feel confident. It's OK. It's going to be all right.

One of the things that we feel as performers is that the physical experience of reading the poem aloud opens some dimension of the poem that we don't always get in silent reading. Do you feel that way when you perform your own poems? Do other dimensions open up?

For me, there's something that keeps me from feeling very much of a gap here. The writing of the poem is so much internalized that my own reading of it seems just right. I mean, there's no difference. So I don't feel I gain, but maybe it's partly because I've already gained. I've already felt it, and heard it, and gone over it, adjusted it, tuned it, so that even if I read it wrong (if there is such a thing for the writer, and there may not be such a thing), it would be accommodated immediately to one of the alternative possibilities when I was writing.

So you think the gain would be greater for the person who had not written the poem.

The gain would be greater, the hazard, and the feeling of difference between what it looks like and what it's going to be when perfected in performance would be there for someone else who was doing it, but it wouldn't be there for me as the writer. I mean, others might sense it, but I wouldn't sense it.

Gary Snyder says he feels readings and recordings of poetry have increased the number of people who listen to poetry and widened the audience in the United States. Do you feel that's true?

Yes, I think readings have. I think more people come to readings and pay attention to a poem there than go to a library in a university and actually read alertly an hour's worth of poetry. I think mostly poets do that. But quite a few go to readings so I do agree with Gary Snyder about that. I think Gary Snyder is a pretty spectacular example of a poet whose place in the current scene depends pretty largely on certain elements of poetry. He's a guru. Physically he's an impressive person, an alive one the way a fish or a bird is alive, or a Doberman.

Animated.

An animated person. His part of what has popularized poetry has been the heroic and the leader-spokesman poet. So much so that I recently saw a review by Richard Tillinghast of a Gary Snyder book, and he said—I do violence to his review— that Snyder is so used to being a spokesman, being right, that that's what he is doing; he's not being a poet anymore.

Do you agree with that?

I sort of do. Not just about Snyder, whom I like, but almost everyone who becomes successful gets enticed toward whatever feels the most like success. So it wouldn't be just someone like Snyder; maybe anybody who's successful begins to go on that foot.

Do you think the media have any potential for developing audiences for poetry? What about National Public Radio?

Well, this is a characteristic weakness of mine, I think, but the first thing that occurs to me is that what happens when poetry goes on television is that it becomes accommodated to television. I think most people's experience of poetry on television distorts poetry.

What about radio? You know they say the pictures are better on radio.

Somehow I feel less jumpy about the effect on radio. For one thing, I don't think people carry their lust for overdoing it into radio the way they do into television. Television has got to pedal faster and faster to keep from falling off. But radio doesn't seem so hazardous. That's just one way to look at it, but that kind of audience that comes to poetry by way of television is the kind of audience that comes to tap dancing, or you know, whatever is going on. I think it's hard. I think the relation, an adequate relation to poetry, requires something that is some kind of experience that is neutralized or cancelled by some of the wave that hits the viewer in television. Maybe I'm speaking partly as a person who's participated in television programs, but when you do it you realize how false it is. There are things you can do and can't do on camera, and there are ways to look, and there are long delays, and you've got to be cut off at a certain time, and there's that presence of the unseen audience all the time that makes you a faker whether you want to be one or not.

Now they have cassette books that you can play in your car as you drive. Would you be willing to record, or to have someone else record, your work for this purpose?

Aside from whether this harmonizes with what I said or not, I feel it might be all right. I feel that a person's involvement in a book, a novel, say, might be enhanced by a good reader. There are people who, when they travel in a car, feel they have to do the driving. I've never felt that way, although I think I'm a good driver and I feel confident. It's within the realm of possibility that there are better drivers than I am, and it's within the realm of possibility that there are better readers than I am. So, I think this would average out for people and that many people, including myself, might get an improved impression of a book from listening to it.

Do you read your own works aloud when you're composing? Do you test the sounds aloud or do you do it mostly mentally?

Well, I want to grab several sentences at once here. One is, mostly mentally. But the other is, there's a relation to language that's between internalizing it and hearing it. When I'm writing I think I'm aware of the sounds of the syllables that I'm writing down, even if I'm writing them silently. So the actual production for the voice on the air, putting it on the air, for sound, is obviously one way to participate with the sound, but there are other ways to participate with sound, I think. As a writer, I'm aware of sound; put it that way. That's the opposite of my first statement—that it's mostly intellectual, mental. But also it's aesthetic, tactile.

Maybe it's kind of like a musician reading a score. He can hear the music even though he's reading silently.

Yes, I've always been awed by musicians who could do that, but I guess as a reader I do that. I hear the notes.

Is there anything you'd like to add to the discussion?

That's a challenge. Well, I've said that you've raised some issues or pushed some issues farther than have happened to me before in these interchanges. I like to get a lot out of these encounters; I think I have for this time. Your way of coming at it is distinctive enough to raise some topics that aren't often raised; or maybe never before for me. These are the mechanical things of possible relation to what a writer is doing. There are extremes in attitudes toward reading poetry among poets themselves. Many immediately go into a different tonality and pace when they read poetry. Then there are others, and I think I would be an extreme on the other side. People have told me often at my readings that they can't tell when I'm reading a poem and when I'm saying something in between the poems. Now, it's possible for me to take this in several ways; but mostly I just understand that. I think my way of telling a poem is to tell it. I think Robert Frost said, "I'll tell you a poem," or "I'll say you a poem," or something like that. Poetry, it seems to me, comes right out of talk; and any extreme departure from the strength of daily conversation—though it may fascinate or excite for a time—will pall and finally strike us as mannered and weak. Even so eloquent a speaker as Dylan Thomas is flourishing by means of a consistent recurrence of bonuses that lurk in speech. "The tradition of total experience" is a phrase that helps me identify my allegiances: in art I find my way by means of all experience, not just those that have been extracted and called the tradition of art.

UNDER DISCUSSION
David Lehman, General Editor
Donald Hall, Founding Editor

Volumes in the Under Discussion series collect reviews and essays about individual poets. The series is concerned with contemporary American and English poets about whom the consensus has not yet been formed and the final vote has not been taken. Titles in the series include: